Learning:
what matters to children

An alphabet of what learners do

Diane Rich
Mary Jane Drummond
Cathy Myer

with contributions from the **What Matters to Children** team

Foreword by Gareth Malone

Published in 2008 by
Rich Learning Opportunities
The Brambles
Manor Road
Clopton
Suffolk
IP13 6SH
United Kingdom

www.richlearningopportunities.co.uk

ISBN 978-0-9549683-1-1

British Library Cataloguing in Publication Data
A catalogue for this title is available from The British Library

Layout and design by Dave Cousins. email dc.bass@yahoo.co.uk
Printed by Expression, IP23 8HH, UK

Additional copies are available from Rich Learning Opportunities

www.richlearningopportunities.co.uk ● ph +44 (0)1473 737405 ● fax +44 (0)1473 737613

CONTENTS

Acknowledgements

We would like first of all to acknowledge the important contributions made by Denise Casanova, Andrea Durrant and Emma Hertzberg who were part of the thinking behind the book in its early stages and provided valuable ideas and learning stories.

We were privileged to have had feedback from all members of the **What Matters to Children** team. In addition to the three authors, the **What Matters to Children** team includes Denise Casanova, Jacqui Cousins, Andrea Durrant, Emma Hertzberg, Jennie Lindon, Marjorie Ouvry, Sue Pearson and Jane Turner. We are grateful to them all for their constructive comments and generous support.

It was a pleasure to work with Dave Cousins to whom we are very grateful for his work in translating our ideas into visual form.

We are grateful to the children and educators we have talked to and observed during the writing of this book and who have inspired us over the years. It is not possible to name them all but we are hugely indebted to them.

Many people from several institutions have made a significant impact on the book, helping us with their insights and additional materials. A wide range of schools and settings are referred to throughout the book. None are identified or described individually as some educators and children preferred to remain anonymous. We are grateful to everyone involved.

The authors and publisher would like to thank the following for permission to include items in this book:
- Bloodaxe Books, Northumberland for permission to include part of the poem, *Relearn The Alphabet* by Denise Levertov.
- The children who allowed us to reproduce their drawings or tell their learning stories, and the schools that gave us permission.

We would also like to thank Elaine Gissing for her invaluable support behind the scenes.

And finally we wish to thank our partners, John Messenger, John Myer and Christopher Towndrow, for their support, encouragement and cheerfulness throughout the writing of this book.

The authors

The authors are experienced and well-respected education consultants. They are all members of the **What Matters to Children** team, co-ordinated by **Rich Learning Opportunities**. They have come together to work on a variety of projects for many years, and have always been committed to promoting *what matters to children.*

Diane Rich is co-author of *First hand experience: what matters to children.* Diane runs **Rich Learning Opportunities**: keeping creativity, play and first hand experience at the heart of children's learning. She co-ordinates the **What Matters to Children** team. Over the years Diane has worked with children as play worker, teacher, advisory teacher, researcher, consultant, author and trustee for children's charities. She works on many projects across the UK and appears on Teachers' TV.

Mary Jane Drummond is co-author of *First hand experience: what matters to children.* Mary Jane is a writer, teacher and researcher with an abiding interest in young children's learning. She has recently retired from the Faculty of Education at the University of Cambridge.

Cathy Myer is co-author of *First hand experience: what matters to children.* Cathy was formerly a teacher, advisory teacher and university lecturer. She is now a freelance consultant, passionate about children and their capacity to learn from their experiences of the real world.

A note about terms

Throughout this book we use the term **we** to refer to the authors.

We use the term **educator** to refer all those who work in a professional capacity with children from birth to 11: carers, childminders, play workers, nursery nurses, teachers, teaching assistants, students. **Teacher** and **childminder** are used in some learning stories.

We use the term **school** to refer to permanent locations where educators work with children, including maintained schools, independent schools, non-maintained and special schools.

We use the term **setting** to refer to any out-of-home provider for children from birth to 11.

Learning stories have come from schools and settings from rural, urban and city based areas of both social deprivation and privilege. Some come from schools with children from a wide range of cultures, and others from monocultural settings.

All those who are significant carers for children at home are referred to as **parents**.

Foreword

Lighting fires
by Gareth Malone

Learning. What is it exactly? I have learnt that 2+2=4. I just *know* it does. I also *understand* that 2+2=4. But furthermore I know that 2+2 *never* equals 5 because I've made that mistake and I'm not going to make it again. I also know that if 2+2=4 then 4-2=2. And that means I can do maths. If I've learnt how to do one sum surely I can do another and another and so on.

A pre-packaged lesson is simply a watered down version of someone else's experience. Hearing it second hand is never as powerful as the first time you mess up big-time – *on your own.* Nobody likes a know-it-all telling you what to do - but everybody turns to somebody older and wiser when they reach the limits of their own knowledge and experience. The teacher and parent tread an impossible tightrope between these opposites. Sometimes the child listens to a throw away comment and acts on it – much to your chagrin. Sometimes you try in vain to 'teach them a lesson' and it goes in one ear… no wait… it doesn't even go in the ear.

Thinking back to my own primary school days I remember the thrilling sense of freedom as we went orienteering on a Shropshire estate. We were largely unsupervised and it was a revelation to me. The necessity to work as a team became imperative. The need to communicate, concentrate, deliberate, plan, self motivate… the list goes on. The sense of personal power and control over my own destiny was immense – *we could have been stranded out there forever.* (In reality we were on a secluded estate with teachers everywhere, hiding up trees - invisibly supervising.) And, every minute of the time, we were learning.

As an adult I've spent my whole career working with young people to help them develop their own creative work and skills. In my work with opera companies I have facilitated the writing of over 200 songs with children; some of them good, some of them bad – but all of them belong to the children, who speak of their own experience in their own voice. I have seen them take responsibility for the writing and performance of dramatic operas of depth and surprising candour. There is inherent risk in not knowing what will happen, handing over the outcomes to them, but this is what excites them. They know that learning, which they do full-time, is the biggest adventure they'll ever go on.

Musicians go on learning all their lives, learning from those younger who have different talents and approaches, learning new music and learning new ways to interpret the great works. Learning and sharing learning are essential tools for a musician who wants to get work. Why do we learn? Not only because we have a deadline (a concert platform with tickets sold) but also because we have an unquenchable thirst for new music and experience. Musicians follow their noses into musical areas that are hitherto uncharted – like polar explorers. So do the children in our schools – if they are given the proper opportunities.

The realities of teaching are that while there are targets to be met, levels to attain and a timetable to adhere to, there are also choices to be made. This book is hugely sympathetic to the needs, pressures and decisions of educators. It offers inspiration and a healthy reminder to us all of the responsibility we have as educators not just to 'light fires' in children's intellects, but to respond, every day, to their life-long addiction to learning.

Gareth Malone
Music animateur and singer
from BBC2's 'The Choir'

Part one
Introduction

What is this book?

This book is both a continuation and a development of the approach we described in our first book, *First hand experience: what matters to children* which we saw as a springboard from which educators and children could launch themselves into the beautiful, challenging, physical world in which we all live. We had been concerned by our observations of schools and other settings for young children, where opportunities for authentic, engaging first hand experiences were few and far between. Our response was to write a sequence of alphabet pages, from *A is for apple* to *Z is for zigzag*, that would support educators in ensuring that children more actively, and more frequently, encounter and explore the living world, and everything and everyone in it.

We also included a variety of 'learning stories', educators' accounts of children learning from first hand experiences, to illustrate our argument that the closer children can get to the real world, looking and listening, touching and tasting, breathing it in, the more worthwhile their learning will be. In further support of this central theme, we included, on every page, short memorable quotations from an eclectic range of thinkers whose work is important to us.

Looking back...

In the two years since the publication of this resource, we have encountered other stimulating writers and texts that emphasise and extend our argument for the necessity of first hand experience as the basis for worthwhile learning. One such message is to be found in a powerful essay on practice at Black Mountain College. Edmund de Waal (2005) quotes extensively from what he calls the 'magisterial' book *On Weaving* by Anni Albers, wife of Josef Albers and leader of the weaving programme at the college. He explains how her teaching was based on her conviction that we have grown increasingly insensitive to our tactile sense. She writes,

> *No wonder a faculty that is so largely unemployed in our daily plodding and bustling is degenerating... Unless we are specialised producers, our contact with materials is rarely more than a contact with the finished product. We remove a cellophane wrapping and there it is – the bacon, or the razor blade, or the pair of nylons...*

This heart-felt reproach, this lament for the loss of contact with the natural, material world, is vividly expressed,

> *Our materials come to us already ground and chipped and powdered and mixed and sliced, so that only the finale in the long sequence of operations from matter to product is left to us: we merely toast the bread. No need to get our hands into the dough.* quoted in de Waal 2006:65

What a splendid contrast: the person whose hands merely toast the bread is revealed as empoverished beside the person whose hands are deep in the dough – a person who touches the world for an authentic purpose, who knows what it is to become intimate with the stuff of the world.

Our book *First hand experience: what matters to children* and follow up work with educators, encouraged educators to offer children opportunities to do likewise, to do more than remove the cellophane wrapping and toast the bread, to learn about the world with their hands in the dough, so to speak.

But in this book for educators of children from birth to 11 we have a different purpose, although we continue to build on the elements represented on the alphabet pages of the first book:

- what matters to children
- big ideas
- the metaphor of food and exercise.

We review each of these elements briefly in the sections that follow.

What matters to children

In the years since 1988, when the national curriculum was introduced in England, a whole generation of teachers and other educators have been invited to think about children's learning in terms of mathematics, English and science, core and foundation subjects, programmes of study, attainment targets, clearly defined objectives, learning intentions, levels 1-5, desirable outcomes, stepping stones. In the 2007 *Statutory Framework for the Early Years Foundation Stage*, the entire early years community in England has been presented with early learning goals, within six areas of learning and development, which

> *...establish expectations for most children to reach by the end of the EYFS.* DfES 2007:12

The four domains of children's learning: what matters to children

But there are other ways of conceptualising children's learning, and we prefer to start with learning that *matters to children,* the learning to which they are spontaneously committed from birth, the learning they pursue throughout the primary years, the learning that is driven by their urgent desire to make sense of the world.

We choose to represent this learning in four inter-related domains of children's spontaneous activity:

being ❦ acting ❦ exploring ❦ thinking

Big ideas

For every topic in *First hand experience: what matters to children*, we show, how when children study small and everyday elements of the world around them (puddles, hairbrushes, hinges, folding chairs, for example), they are also learning to think about big ideas, important ideas that play a significant part in their determined efforts to make sense of the world, how it works and how it can be made a better place for everyone.

In doing this, we were deeply influenced by the work of Susan Isaacs (1885–1948), who introduced a whole generation of educators to the principle that active, enquiring, exploring children are also profound thinkers, grappling with challenging and complex ideas. The children at the *Malting House school, whom Susan Isaacs observed so intently, were doing more than 'getting their hands in the dough', in Annie Albers' terms, more than lighting bonfires, experimenting with weights and pulleys, caring for the pet rabbits, or working in the well-equipped carpentry workshop; they were, she demonstrates, engaged in the processes of reasoning, discovery and thought, working out how and why things happen, gradually building up their understanding of, for example, cause and effect, the relation between form and function, gravity and density, living and non-living things, the cycle of reproduction, life and death.

This element of our approach, children's growing understanding of what we are here calling 'big ideas',

has much in common with the work of Chris Athey and others on persistent patterns in the play and activity of some children from 18 months onwards; these patterns of play reveal the underlying 'cognitive forms' or 'schemas' of their thinking, the big ideas that fascinate them. Athey (1990) describes, as does Cathy Nutbrown (1999), how close observation of children's play can show parents and educators their children's burning interests – in things that go up and down for example, (a vertical dynamic schema), or things that go round and round (a dynamic circular schema). Indeed, the fascination of some two and three year olds with these dynamic schemas is, in a sense, the foundation of a later interest in the big ideas of gravity, flight, distance, space, the vastness of the universe, the movements of the planets, and so on, ideas that can only be understood on the basis of earlier experiences.

Our purpose in doing this, in identifying the big ideas that children encounter in their full-time project of making sense of the world, was to support educators in seeing more clearly the depth and richness of children's learning, helping them to see how much of substance there is to appreciate in children's thinking and doing.

*For a full description of this school, see chapter G.

Food and exercise

More than one writer on child development has used the metaphor of 'food and exercise' to explore the idea of an appropriate curriculum; we adopted this phrase to advocate, first, a rich and nourishing diet of first hand experiences, and secondly, manifold opportunities for children to exercise their growing powers to do, to think, to understand, to represent and express their understanding, to act on the world in ways of their own invention.

Some of the educators to whom we have presented this metaphor as a way of thinking about the quality of their provision, have expressed concerns that it limits their capacity to introduce children to new tools, techniques, physical activities or material resources. Their anxiety is that their adult expertise may constrain the children's own energetic exploration of the world. In response, we emphasise that the expertise and experience of educators are, in a sense, part of the food. Indeed, they are an important part of the diet educators offer, since the introduction of new ways of handling tools, or their own bodies, or mark-making materials, for example, increases children's capacity to act on the world for themselves, far from constraining it.

Since the publication of *First hand experience: what matters to children*, we have come to see how powerful an evaluative tool this metaphor can be. It can help educators think about the quality of the intellectual diet they provide for children: is it rich enough? Sustaining enough? Is there enough for everyone? Do the ideas that children meet matter enough to them? Furthermore, it can help educators think about the opportunities for 'exercise' that they organise for children: do they have enough time, enough space, and enough variety for the strenuous exercise of their intellectual muscles? Which of their growing powers will be strengthened by their daily activities? Are there enough opportunities for them to exercise what Susan Isaacs calls their 'thirst for understanding... a veritable passion'?

...And moving on

In this book, we move on from our concern with the rich curriculum diet that children deserve, to explore more fully the ideas that are implicit in our use of the term exercise as a kind of shorthand for *what learners do*. While on every alphabet page of *First hand experience: what matters to children* we included a number of active verbs (such as: find, investigate, collect, visit, make), which we see as activities that would naturally arise in the study of any particular topic, we did not discuss their significance, or consider how educators can best support and value the characteristic behaviours of active learners. By active learners we mean more than simply busy learners, who spend their days in physical activity, building, climbing, cutting and sticking, speeding around on bicycles, rushing from activity to activity. We want to look a little deeper, and examine the internal processes that characterise the lives of effective learners.

Learning stories

We enrich our text with a variety of 'learning stories', first hand accounts of learners who, in their spontaneous and purposeful activity, play, enquiry and interactions, illustrate the ideas we are examining. The learning stories are intended to underline our central purpose in this book: to demonstrate that looking at *what learners do* is a good way for educators to learn more about learning.

In the main body of the text that follows, we identify a selection of these processes, these ways of being an active learner, and discuss their importance, drawing on our own work with children from birth to 11, our work with educators, our reading, our research, evaluation and development projects.

is for *play*

The **What Matters to Children** team is committed to the importance of play: we see it as a necessary, indispensable part of what effective learners do. But we have not included the verb 'play' as a separate page in our alphabet. Learners **do** play; there can be no disagreement about that. However, we prefer to think of play in its noun form, so that it stands as an umbrella term for all the times and places where play happens; we see play as a site for many different kinds of learning. To say that 'learners play' might suggest that is all they do in the course of their play. This would be nonsense, because, in their play, children exercise all their growing powers to do, to think, to feel, to understand, to represent and express. In their play, up a tree, or under a bush, alone or with their friends, children belong, choose, explore, hope, imagine, make meaning, make stories, represent their thinking, and so much more.

Two authors whose work we discuss later in the book, Debra Van Ausdale and Joe Feagin, share our view of the central importance of play in children's learning; they argue that children making sense of the world through play deserve to be taken very seriously. But, they comment,

> ... 'play' may not be the most accurate English word for this recurring activity of children. What they do is often more serious and adult-like than the term 'play' suggests, especially since the common-sense understanding of play is that it is frivolous, insignificant activity. Indeed, words used with 'play' include 'simple', 'easy' and 'naïve'.
>
> 2001:24

In this text then, we have chosen to represent children learning through their play on many pages, throughout the book, in order to honour the significant and serious purposes of this pervasive aspect of *what learners do*.

A map of the book: the richness of what learners do

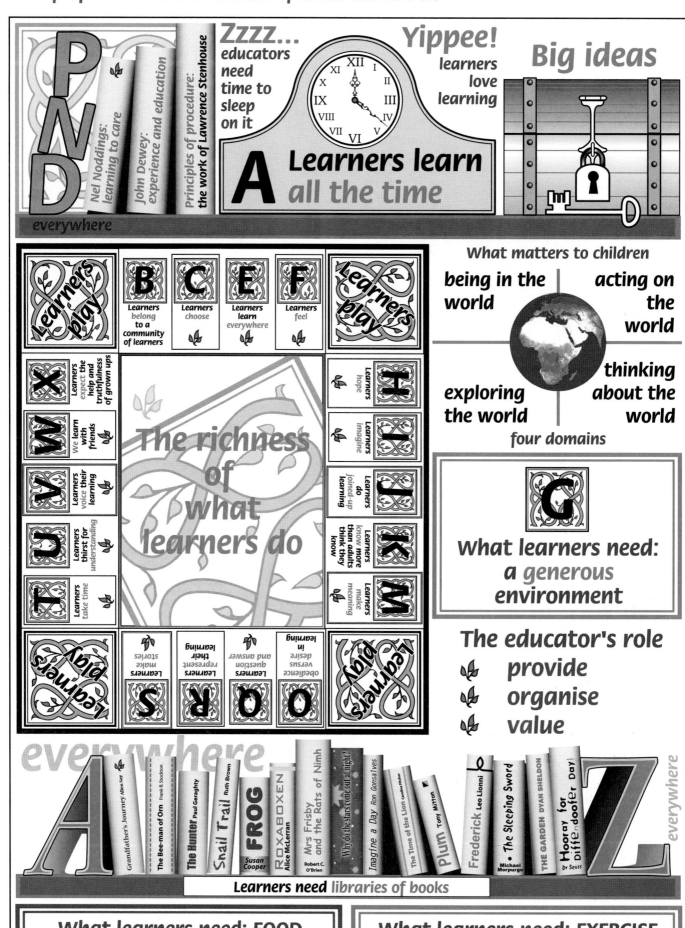

P N D — *everywhere*

Nel Noddings: learning to care

John Dewey: experience and education

Principles of procedure: the work of Lawrence Stenhouse

Zzzz... educators need time to sleep on it

Yippee! learners love learning

A Learners learn all the time

Big ideas

What matters to children

being in the world | acting on the world

exploring the world | thinking about the world

four domains

B — Learners belong to a community of learners

C — Learners choose

E — Learners learn everywhere

F — Learners feel

Learners play

The richness of what learners do

H — Learners hope

I — Learners imagine

J — Learners do joined-up learning

K — Learners know more than adults think they know

M — Learners make meaning

X — Learners expect the help and truthfulness of grown ups

W — We learn with friends

V — Learners voice their learning

U — Learners thirst for understanding

T — Learners take time

S — Learners make stories

R — Learners represent their learning

Q — Learners question and answer

O — obedience versus desire in learning

G what learners need: a generous environment

The educator's role
- provide
- organise
- value

everywhere

A ... Z everywhere

Grandfather's Journey *Allen Say*
The Bee-man of Orn *Frank R. Stockton*
The Hunter *Paul Geraghty*
Snail Trail *Ruth Brown*
FROG *Susan Cooper*
ROXABOXEN *Alice McLerran*
Mrs Frisby and the Rats of Nimh *Robert C. O'Brien*
Why do the stars come out at night?
Imagine a Day *Ron Gonsalves*
The Time of the Lion *Caroline Pitcher*
Plum *Tony Mitton*
Frederick *Leo Lionni*
The Sleeping Sword *Michael Morpurgo*
THE GARDEN *DYAN SHELDON*
Hooray for Diffendoofer Day! *Dr Seuss*

Learners need libraries of books

What learners need: FOOD for their learning

What learners need: EXERCISE for their growing powers

A map of the book: the richness of what learners do

The map of the book shows its different elements. The main body of the alphabet book consists of 21 chapters about *what learners do,* which include learning stories, first hand accounts of children in action. There are three chapters (corresponding to the three letters D, N and P) which take the form of short essays on writers whose work seems especially relevant to a consideration of *what learners do*: John Dewey, Nel Noddings and Lawrence Stenhouse. We have not attempted to give comprehensive accounts of the entire life's work of these eminent thinkers. We see these pages as a way of opening doors, as it were, onto ideas and approaches that may be unfamiliar, but that we believe merit a closer acquaintance.

At the end of every chapter from B to Y, there is an outline of one relevant book for educators and one for children. The children's books vary in style; there are picture books, novels, poetry and information books. They have been chosen for big ideas that children will encounter, not with a particular reading age in mind. The big ideas in a picture book can be as relevant to an older reader as they are to very young children, and a long novel, which can be read chapter by chapter, can be relevant to children of many different ages.

Chapters A and Z are different again: A contains a fairy tale for educators, and Z, the final chapter, is a review of the main themes of the book, which remain constant through the whole volume.

Linking learning

Many books have been written about learners and aspects of learning, books that have focused on imagination, representation, story making and play, for example. This book, however, explores learning as a whole, both from the child's point of view, and from the educators' in terms of the choices they might make in their provision. In this book we focus on what learners actually **do**, the verbs of learning, active children belonging, choosing, feeling and representing and so on. In every chapter we consider a single verb of learning, but each of these, stitched together with play, links with other verbs to make a joined up, worthwhile whole.

What is this book for?

As we have already explained, the purpose of this book is to examine closely the characteristics of effective learners, to describe the internal processes that accompany the play, exploration, enquiry and talk of active learners. But it is also important to make clear what the book is not about, what we are not trying to do.

We are not trying to do educators' thinking for them. We are not telling them what to think. We are not offering an alternative curriculum framework, or practical guidance on how to interpret current national and local frameworks. We are committed to the principle of educators who think for themselves, making choices that will ensure worthwhile learning, *learning that matters to children.*

So this is a book for educators of children from birth to 11 to think with.

To think about what, precisely?

About children as learners, about what learners do.

An objection!

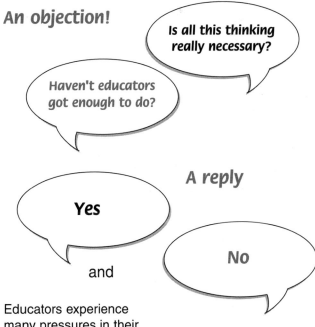

Is all this thinking really necessary?

Haven't educators got enough to do?

A reply

Yes

and

No

Educators experience many pressures in their busy professional lives. They operate within frameworks not of their own choosing; they have to make these work in the interests of children's learning.

We realise that any kind of curriculum framework imposes constraints of some kind or another. However, we firmly believe that the current frameworks offer educators manifold opportunities to make wise choices and informed decisions.

Our argument is that these choices and decisions need thinking about. This book is designed to support that thinking.

We believe that in thinking about the most appropriate curriculum and pedagogy for children from birth to 11, the best place for educators to start is with the children themselves, the people who do the learning.

How can educators use this book?

The 21 chapters of this book that focus on *what learners do*, illustrated with learning stories, are designed to heighten educators' awareness of these particular aspects of being a learner. Reading about children learning – belonging, choosing, feeling, imagining, making meaning, and so on – will, we hope, help educators see more clearly and more completely the richness of *what learners do*. So these chapters can be used to enrich educators' thinking about children's learning.

These chapters can also be used to support educators in reviewing the quality of their provision for all the different things that learners do. They will help them see more clearly the consequences of the choices they make, and more accurately evaluate the worthwhileness of the learning that happens all the time in their settings.

The three chapters of the book that focus on the thinkers and writers Dewey, Noddings and Stenhouse, have a similar purpose: to support educators' thinking. Furthermore, they show how, in every period of educational history, there are always alternatives to the official position or traditional approach, different priorities, different ways of seeing, thinking, planning and reviewing. These three chapters could be used, we suggest, as the basis of discussion and debate, as educators in small groups, or in solitary study, try to clarify for themselves the principles on which they base their own priorities, choices and decisions about their practice. Because whatever the current curriculum framework, educators still make choices and decisions for themselves.

Why should educators of children from birth to 11 use this book?

Because it will help them

- to become familiar with the four domains of children's learning: what matters to children

- to become familiar with the theme of big ideas in children's learning; to become confident in observing, identifying and documenting children's growing understanding of them

- to become familiar with the theme of food and exercise; to become confident in using it as a tool for planning and critical reflection on practice

- to become familiar with the richness of all that learners do when they are offered a nourishing, stimulating diet, and given manifold opportunities for intellectual and social exercise

- to appreciate the importance of play as one of the most significant aspects of what learners do

- to understand and appreciate their own powers to make wise choices and good decisions in the interests of children

- to be stimulated and supported in doing the important kinds of thinking that characterise the effective educator

  thinking about children

  about curriculum

  and about learning.

This is the thinking that underpins every aspect of provision for worthwhile learning.

Part two

An alphabet of what learners do

What do learners do?
Learners learn all the time

and here is a fairy story to illustrate this simple proposition

The Sleeping Beauty
[rewritten]

Not the whole story, but an extract from quite near the beginning – let's say at the middle of the beginning.

*The king and queen
who grieved so deeply for their
childlessness have become the proud parents
of a lovely baby girl, who (as we all know)
will grow up to be the Sleeping Beauty.
But first comes the christening,
the banquet, the baby in her royal cradle,
and the godparents standing by to present
their gifts. Now is the moment for the first
good fairy to step forward and say,
"I give you the gift of being a passionate
learner, eager to understand the world."*

*Then the second good fairy, in her turn,
leans over the cradle, and says,
"I give you the gift of being an imaginative
learner, inventive and creative."*

*The third fairy follows, saying,
"I give you the gift of being a powerful
learner, exploring and enquiring and
making sense for yourself."*

*Now, (as we all know), comes the turn
of the bad fairy, who declares,
"I give you the gift of never being
able to stop learning,
the gift of learning all the time."*

And now of course we can see that this is not a fairy story at all. This is what actually happens when every tiny baby is born. They are all born with all of these gifts, including that of the bad fairy. They are all born with the gift of never being able to stop learning. And the implications of this for educators are simply colossal.

It means that children learn from educators all the time, not just when they are at their best. Children learn on the bad days, when their educators are less than wonderful. They learn from the most engaging and meaningful experiences educators offer, and they learn from the undemanding, meaningless, unprofitable, indifferent ones. Some of the time, some children do the wrong kind of learning. They learn to disengage, to turn off, to tune out; they learn to be bored. They learn how it feels to be excluded, rather than included. They learn the pain of rejection, rather than the joy of belonging and the pleasure of companionship.

In other words, if educators give children the wrong food, curriculum food that isn't nourishing, or the wrong exercise, activities that don't stretch or stimulate them, children will do the wrong kind of learning. They will fail to thrive as learners. And it won't do.

Educators can't allow children to do the wrong kinds of learning; children are too important and the right kinds of learning too precious. And that is why we have written this book; to support educators, all those who work with and for young and primary school aged children, in thinking about their professional responsibility to get the food and exercise right, to provide and organise for the right kind of learning, the *learning that matters to children*. We believe that if educators can keep their collective professional eye on the big over-arching principle of *what matters to children*, they will be able to cope with the bad fairy. They will be able to make absolutely certain that children do the right kind of learning.

🍃 *And because they can, they will.*

What do learners do?
Learners belong to a community of learners

What is it to belong?

Some educators respond, in terms of their own lives both within and outwith their professional settings:

"Feeling accepted by the people around you."

"Being valued."

"Your voice is heard, your opinion is sought."

"Not being left out."

"Having a part to play, knowing what that part is."

"Knowing your way around, being confident to do so."

"Sharing beliefs – and sharing practices, routines, special events."

"People wait to hear what you have to say."

"Knowing the ropes, the rules of the game."

"It's simple – it's just doing things together."

The work of Vivian Gussin Paley

In one of her early books, *Wally's Stories* (1981), Vivian Gussin Paley, already an experienced kindergarten teacher, describes the first time she used the technique for which she is now so well known: acting out children's dictated stories. Although in previous classes she had encouraged story dictation, it had been in her own words 'a minor activity', even though story books and dramatic play had been high-priority activities. She had come to accept that only a few children in her class, most often girls, enjoyed dictating stories. But one day, Wally dictates this fine dinosaur story.

> *The dinosaur smashed down the city and the people got mad and put him in jail.*
> *"Is that the end?" I asked. "Did he get out?"*
> *He promised he would be good so they let him go home and his mother was waiting.*

And on the spot, Paley decides to invite him to act out his very own story, just as before when they had acted out fairy tales, story books, poems and songs. The result was unexpected.

> *It made Wally very happy and a flurry of story writing began that continued and grew all year. The boys dictated as many stories as the girls and we acted out each story the day it was written.*

> *Before we had never acted out these stories... it had always seemed enough just to write the children's words. Obviously it was not; the words did not sufficiently represent the action, which needed to be shared. For this alone the children would give up play time, as it was a true extension of play.*   p.12

The simple acting out, by the children, of their own stories within a circle of their classmates, became the central activity of each day; stories about the children's acted-out stories feature in each of Paley's successive books.

Twenty years on from the publication of *Wally's Stories*, Paley spoke at a conference in London hosted by London Bubble, a thriving experimental theatre company, which has taken up Paley's approach and used it extensively in early years settings and in-school training sessions. Paley's presentation, 'How children invent community through their stories and play', was a distillation of her philosophy and practice. She centred her thoughts around her most recent book, *In Mrs. Tully's Room* (2001) then still in press, which describes the story telling and acting out of two year old children in a remarkable childcare centre.

'How children invent community through their stories and play'

The text that follows is an edited version of notes taken at the 2001 conference; it shows how close, for Paley, are the concepts of story telling, community and belonging.

I am going to talk about how play and story are the basis of community...

The stories have to be acted out, on the stage. They are not private conversations, but public discussions of important events with common significance.

Community is seen and felt when fantasy weaves us into a common story.

There is only one problem with children's play - and this is where theatre comes in. [We have] this wonderful play, from which everything else stems, for the rest of our lives, but not everyone can participate in every play, in the large group, in the great play. The answer is theatre.

There needs to be a structure - in the play, for the play, of the play, for the whole community. The play is a metaphor for inclusion, for what it means for the rest of our lives.

Everyone, everyday, listens to five or six or more stories. The more stories the better. The more voices the better.

From the beginning, every child deserves an audience. Every child deserves to be listened to. Everyone has a story; every story is fascinating; every story must be listened to: this is one of the great lessons that must be learned.

No-one is kept out of telling a story. No-one is kept out of acting a story: these are good rules for life.

Extracts from In Mrs. Tully's Room: a childcare portrait

In Mrs. Tully's room, [there is] a literary network, propelled by the need children have to connect themselves to one another through their plays and stories. Mrs. Tully calls it community, but it is also theatre...

"When my babies do their stories," Mrs. Tully had told me, "they really see each other. That's what we need to go after in school, the seeing and the listening to each other."

pp.14, 23

Knowing the ropes

One aspect of belonging is the feeling of 'knowing the ropes', 'knowing your way around', or even just knowing 'the rules of the game'. Can this form of belonging be promoted in early years settings and primary schools?

In a mixed age class nine, ten and eleven year olds are learning what it is to be members of a community, 'a team', a term their class teacher, Narinder, often uses. She demonstrates the principle of solidarity to them, emphasising that she is a member of the same community, that she is on their side; they learn the lesson of solidarity with one another. For Narinder, her pupils' learning is necessarily related to their social relationships: it is by living together that they learn.

> *As they walk through the door, they must have a sense of belonging. The school is theirs; decisions are taken by them, not for them... They have to feel that it's their environment [the classroom]... They are the ones who make the rules and charters about what is acceptable. They are the ones who organise the classroom in the way they feel is best... They make the decisions, they decide... on rules, rights and responsibilities.*
>
> Hart et al 2004:90

Narinder is convinced that the learning that follows from the pupils' work on these aspects of their lives in school is of greater importance than their learning from the statutory subject areas.

What about younger children? Can they be involved in the same way?

In another primary school, the staff collaborated in a partnership research study, examining 'positive alternatives to exclusion' (Cooper et al 2000). The staff group had just completed a year-long project to draw up a behaviour policy, emphasising the quality of relationships. The final document contains a section on bullying, and how it will be treated; there is a fascinating list that defines bullying behaviour, which includes these items:

- *sniggering or eyeballing when someone else is in trouble*
- *playing lurgy games*
- *putting notes in people's trays.*

No teacher wrote this list! It is the pupils' voices that are speaking here, with the authority of experience. There is more to being bullied than suffering from highly visible and violent assaults, or the growing trend for phone and internet bullying; lurgy games too are painful and cannot be tolerated. In another list, detailing 20 aspects of unacceptable behaviour, there is a similar respect for the sensitivity of children of all ages from four to 11. The pupils who are on the receiving end of petty, trivial acts of unkindness are the experts in their own condition; they are prepared to name the behaviours they will not accept, and stand by the rules they have themselves drawn up.

In our school it is unacceptable to:

armlock

headlock

whip people with clothes or bags

lift people up

stop people going to the toilet

Selected items from the behaviour policy
Cooper et al 2000: 25

The behaviour policy at this school takes account of children's perceptions (including those of the very youngest) of what makes a harmonious community, where everyone is safe from eyeballing and armlocks. As a result, staff and children all agree, the policy and its implementation have made a difference to the quality of everybody's lives together.

Octopus class rules

Not all sets of school and classroom rules have the same power to promote a sense of belonging. The rules listed below were observed in a class of four and five year olds in 2002.

In Octopus class we:
- · **keep in our own space**
- · **keep our classroom tidy**
- · **play nicely with our friends**
- · **work hard**
- · **listen carefully**

This is no framework for fostering young children's spontaneous acts of friendship and community. Under this rule of law, children are discouraged from moving close to one another, or discovering the passions of friendship, quarrelling and peace-making; they are encouraged to listen silently rather than to tell astonishing stories or imagine new and impossible worlds. Belonging to a tidy classroom is no substitute for belonging to a community of learners.

nokcw

A class of five year old children was discussing good rules that would help them live together as a community. They drew pictures and wrote the rules beside them. The rules were authentic, essential and very specific: there were no vague generalisations.

One boy felt it necessary to write and illustrate the following rule:

[no kicking willies]

Harmony: being engaged with an authentic purpose

Early one spring Mr. Morton, who lived in a small rural village, discovered an aged cider press at an auction of old farm implements. He bought it and restored it to full working order. That year there was a particularly good crop of apples and Mr. Morton invited villagers with apple trees to join his Cider Pressing Club.

In September, wheelbarrows were filled with apples and trundled along to Mr Morton's garden where the press sat in its newly restored glory.

Then the cider making began. First the apples had to be washed by four and six year olds Sam and Jess. Then the fruit was 'scratted' by Jack, aged eight, in the scratting machine, a fearsome device that split the apples. Next Jack's father, Mark, shredded the scratted fruit, which was then fed into the press by other villagers.

There was joy as the first trickle of golden juice flowed down the tube into the demijohn, carefully guided by Sam. Children happily sampled the pure apple juice. Later, after fermentation, adults enjoyed their cider.

Children and adults had worked together to make the apple juice and cider. Everybody had had a part to play. There was mutual interest in the process, pride in the product and respect for one another.

Te Whāriki

The bilingual document from New Zealand, *Te Whāriki: Early Childhood Curriculum* outlines a framework from which educators across the whole range of early childhood settings can construct their own versions of an early years curriculum. They all work from the same four agreed principles, and five 'strands' of learning and development. One of these strands is **BELONGING**, described as follows.

Children and their families feel a sense of belonging

Goals
Children and their families experience an environment where:

- *connecting links with the family and the wider world are affirmed and extended*

- *they know that they have a place*

- *they feel comfortable with the routines, customs, and regular events*

- *they know the limits and boundaries of acceptable behaviour.*
  Ministry of Education 1996:15

Later in the document, these four goals are given extensive explication (over eight pages of text), which outlines detailed learning outcomes, in terms of knowledge, skills and attitudes, examples of experiences which lead towards these outcomes, and some stimulating 'Questions for Reflection'. One of these is well worth thinking about:

> **What aspects of the environment help children feel that this is a place where they belong?**

Belonging to a harmonious community

Jane Lane, advocate worker for racial equality in the early years, writes eloquently about the word 'harmonious'.

> *Over recent years, in the field of 'race relations', this word has become associated somewhat negatively and sentimentally with concepts of people living side by side but not really fully communicating with, understanding or accepting one another. This is because the inequalities structured into our society caused by racism are not addressed. I believe 'harmonious' should be reclaimed as a positive word whose origins are in music – the various instruments or voices playing together, in their differing roles, to create a harmony of sound, each contributing equally to the whole. In such harmony, there is no hierarchy between the instruments or voices, each complementing the other(s) and uniting together to make a totality more profound that the individual parts.* 2006:5

Right From The Start

This is the title of the publication from which the quotation above is taken, a powerful document, dentifying priority issues for action in the field of racial equality, setting these issues clearly 'within the context of an integrated approach to all the diverse aspects and inequalities of our society.' It analyses the sources of inequality, identifies obstacles to countering it, and goes on to suggest contributions that could be made by everyone in the early years community (all workers, children and their families) to the fostering of a sense of belonging.

In early years settings, argues Lane, educators are well-placed to play a part in creating a more harmonious society. This stage in children's lives is a critical opportunity for their learning.

> *...learning to appreciate each other equally and to be positive about those who are different from themselves, as well as recognising the many similarities. There is an opportunity to learn from each other, to be open and broad minded, to share experiences and to feel comfortable within each other's cultural backgrounds, not feeling threatened by cultural diversity, but welcoming it as a fact of life.*
> pp.5-6

Again and again, Lane emphasises that a harmonious society, where everyone belongs, will not come about by chance: it needs to be planned for.

> *The earliest years of children's lives provide a crucial starting point for the process of breaking down the barriers which prevent everyone in our society from participating fully in what it has to offer and developing a sense of belonging.*
>
> p.9

In a later section, 'Priority Issues For Action', Lane sets out necessary actions at a variety of levels, ministerial, departmental, local authority and at the level of early years settings themselves. One of these last recommendations most beautifully describes the community of learners that we are advocating in these pages:

> *transforming settings into havens of security, peace, refuge, support and empathy for all – in other words as microcosms of an ideal world.*
>
> p.27

Questions worth asking about a school or setting

Who belongs here?
Imagine some children's answers....

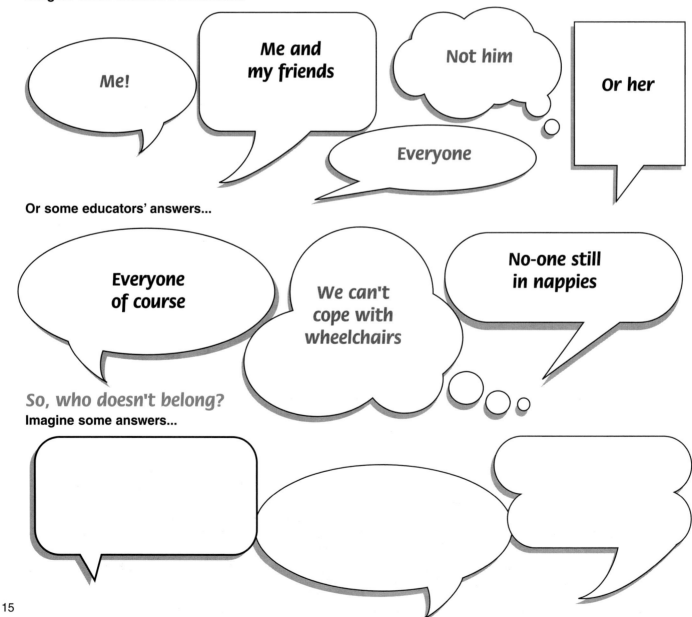

Or some educators' answers...

So, who doesn't belong?
Imagine some answers...

The centrality of belonging

In our educational experience, participation – that is feeling a part and having a sense of belonging – is a value and quality of the school as a whole.   Rinaldi 2006:140

A book for children

Grandfather's Journey

by Allen Say

In this book children encounter the complexity of belonging to two places at the same time. Allen Say's grandfather spent his life between two countries, America and Japan, never entirely at home in either, yet belonging to both.

This beautifully illustrated book explores the longing and restlessness of three generations of a family who have a home in two places.

Big ideas:	identity
	home
	belonging

A book for educators

In Mrs Tully's Room

by Vivian Gussin Paley

This is perhaps the finest of all Vivian Gussin Paley's books ... except of course for *White Teacher* (1979), *Bad Guys Don't have Birthdays* (1988), *You Can't Say You Can't Play* (1992), *The Girl with the Brown Crayon* (1997), *A Child's Work* (2004)... it's clearly impossible to decide.

Mrs. Tully is director and headteacher of a childcare centre in Chicago for two, three and four year old children, who leave her small setting for one year in kindergarten before they enter first grade and formal education. In Mrs. Tully's room children do what Mrs. Tully calls 'the real academics of the early years: language and sensible thinking and good play and a love of stories.' On top of all that, they do community and belonging, simply through being friends and sharing their stories. They live together in harmony; Paley's account of this extraordinary centre is, in itself, extraordinary – moving, challenging, inspiring, humbling – and studded with those

...magical moments in a classroom when everyone floats together on the same cloud.

p.125

Review

These are main themes of chapter B.

- A sense of belonging is central to the well-being that characterises engaged, active learners.
- Children build this sense of belonging through the connections they make with one another through their play and their shared stories.
- Children understand very well the factors that contribute to the harmonious society to which they want to belong: they can help their educators to establish rules and routines that promote a sense of belonging.
- A harmonious society, where everyone belongs, will not come about by chance. Educators and children have to work together to achieve it.

What do learners do?
Learners *choose*

Choosing starts early

Charlie is eight months old and has started to crawl. His father reflects on his ability to make choices. "He definitely has favourite toys and fads. His favourite toys at the moment are his blue shakers. He saw me playing them last week – I picked them up to play along to a pop song and he loved it. Ever since then it's what he wants. When he comes into this room it's what he looks for. He wades through his other toys to get them."

Without his father showing him how the shakers are used, Charlie would probably not have been so determined to play with them himself. He had been given them a few weeks ago, he handled them briefly whenever he came across them, but now he is fired with determination to get hold of the shakers.

Charlie is beginning to make choices: choices that matter to him.

Wise words from Christian Schiller

But we are not able to choose unless we have not only the opportunity to choose but also the capacity, the power to make a choice… We are born utterly helpless with no capacity for choice, but from birth the capacity to choose begins to grow and grow quickly, and like all human powers it grows with exercise.   1979:76

Exercise in choosing

Even before they can crawl, babies can choose. Anita Hughes (2006) celebrates the work of Elinor Goldschmied as the pioneer of Treasure Baskets, developed in the 1940s. Hughes recommends Treasure Baskets as a way of offering choices to babies, especially those who cannot move independently to reach objects. Treasure Baskets, low, sturdy, woven baskets, are filled with a glorious variety of objects, natural, recycled, household things, each just big enough for a sitting-up baby to pick up and handle.

Hughes describes the objects in a Treasure Basket as 'food for the brain' providing new sensory experiences, mental stimulation and satisfaction: in addition, this nourishing food provides babies with the exercise of choosing.

"Do this, this way"

The act of choosing is central to being a learner. Without choice children follow a path laid down by someone else.
"Do this, this way."
 "These are the tools you will use."
  "This is the solution to this problem."
   "This is what you think."

To choose to play, what, where, and with whom, to choose to write because there is a desire and a purpose to do so, to make choices in finding solutions to problems, to choose appropriate tools and materials, to choose to represent thinking, feeling and experience in a variety of ways – in all these choices, children express purpose, control and ownership.

To choose wisely who to spend time with, to choose between good and bad, right and wrong, fair and unfair, wise and unwise, compassionate and hurtful, sensitive and insensitive – in all these choices, children build their own world maps and moral maps.

Each time children make a choice they exercise their power over the world they live in. They live by the outcomes of their choices and so add another piece of learning to their developing understanding of the world and the way it works.

Slip, slide, slip

John, aged nine wrote and illustrated his poem, *My Pond*. He had watched this drama unfold and wanted to record it in a way that expressed the slow stalking movement of the cat towards its prey. John wrote the poem with an audience in mind and chose his design with care. He knew that the form would give impact to the words, that it would lead his audience to enjoy his sharp wit at the poem's end.

In Schiller's terms, John had both the opportunity and the power to realise his poem.

my pond
the sun is shaning on the water A newt plops into it. The cat is watching:

Head swings
Side to side
as newt swims
Side to side
cat licks lip
but starts
to slip
slip
slide
slip
cat takes a dip

8 lines

Provide and organise: what educators can do

When there is a preoccupation with detailed planning for curriculum coverage, there may be fewer opportunities for children to choose: a central aspect of being a learner. Many activities become carefully structured by educators in advance to deliver a learning objective in as few moves as possible. There is so much to do and so little time to do it. Achievement is measured by the number of boxes that have been ticked by the end of a session, a day, or a week. The pressure on educators is intense.

In such a climate, how much choice do children really have?

Trivial choices
Is it only between one colour paper and another?
Or between using felt tip pens or coloured pencils?
Or is choice something that only happens on a Friday during 'choosing time'?
These choices are trivial.

Important choices
Children can make important choices, given the opportunity. If educators themselves exercise their power to choose, children can be given important choices to make, choices that will stimulate significant acts of judgement and reflection. In short, in order for children to be able to increase their capacity to choose, to make informed choices, they need the help

of adults, parents and educators, to provide and organise for choice. Then each setting will become a place where choices are celbrated, encouraged, promoted and valued.

Children exercise their power of choice whenever they act as designers, artists, builders, dancers, musicians, writers, actors, engineers, scientists, inventors and philosophers, but they also need to know how the stuff of their choice will work. Otherwise their capacity to use it will be limited. So children need adults to feed them with this knowledge, modelling and demonstrating a range of options.

As children consider their options they ask themselves questions. From these questions they make decisions. They can then reflect on their actions and ask, "Did I make the right choice, the wisest choice, the most appropriate choice, the best choice at that time? Did it work?"

Providing choices for children... *in making*

a mural

> How do we want it to look?
> What shall we use to make it?

a sculpture

> What will be the best stuff to use? How do we know? Where shall we put it?

a picnic

> Who is it for? What will we need?
> Is it a winter picnic or a summer picnic?

a water garden

> What is it for? Is it for playing in?
> Is it for wildlife?
> What will we put in it?

Providing choices for children... *in solving problems*

> The floor round the water tray gets very slippery: how can we keep the floor dry?

> What vegetables should we plant to make soup every week throughout the winter?

> How do we decide who to invite to our concert when we only have 125 chairs?

What might be a solution?

> What choices do we have?

> How can we try them out?

> Are these the only ways?

> What other ways could there be?

> Which one shall we choose?

What's the best way to keep out the sun?

A class of eight and nine year olds were complaining about their over bright and hot classroom. During the summer term they found it difficult to concentrate with the sun streaming in through the unshaded windows. They discussed the situation with their teacher and decided that what was needed were blinds. They had some choices to consider: the easy choice, to buy ready made blinds or curtains; or a more challenging choice, to make their own. Blinds and curtains were very expensive to buy commercially so they decided to make their own.

The teacher introduced them to the process of making a batik that could be hung on a pole to cover the window throughout the sunny summer days. The process of batik involves making many choices.

Working in self-chosen groups, children made a series of designs. They based them on bees, because of their fascination with a recent classroom installment; a glass-fronted beehive through which they could study the daily lives of bees and the honey-making process.

Children worked individually on their designs and then collaborated to choose which three to use for the blinds. The agreed on one showing a beehive, another a honeycomb, and a third, flowers with

bees. The teacher introduced them to the complex steps in batik making. The children chose colours, yellow and brown as befitted the bees, to dye the cloth. The finished blinds were hung over the windows.

The children evaluated their work:
> Did they keep out the sun?
> Was the classroom more comfortable?
> Had they made wise choices, both practically and aesthetically?
> How would they do it differently next time?
> What had they learned?
> Was it just about the batik process or was it about how they could make a difference to their environment by working together to find a solution?

These children were real designers finding a solution to a problem that affected their environment; it mattered to them. They had to make effective choices. Their suggestions were valued and realised. With the support of their educator they had the capacity to act on their ideas. Because she had introduced the children to a new technique, they were now equipped to choose the medium of batik when they wanted.

Children exercise their choice to play...

In play, children freely choose the activity. The motivation to play comes from within the child, occurring without external demands or rewards. The goals of play are self-imposed rather than imposed by others. Wolfenberg 1999:25

Children of all ages can be ready to play, but easily become disengaged when the play agenda is not their own and the motivation does not come from within them. Texts for educators that use the terms 'well-planned-play', 'adult directed play', 'play with a purpose' and 'structured play' can lead to educators limiting children's choices in play, or worse, turning them off choosing to play altogether.

Educators may spend hours creating exotic role-play areas, then lament that children have not noticed or appreciated their efforts. They despair when children fail to do what is expected of them. Inside an elaborate hairdresser's salon, a tea party develops with enthusiastic mothers and babies; a travel agency is transformed into an unexpected bus to Dinosaur Land, where adventures with terrible lizards are two-a-penny; in a cosy home corner, monsters arrive and take key players away to a cage in a zoo. Robbers and police dogs dominate hospitals, and the house at the top of the beanstalk remains without giants. The children in these episodes of play are making their own choices, playing at *what matters to them.*

And because they can, they will

Despite the demands on educators that appear to reduce their capacity to create arenas in which children can make worthwhile choices, the good news is that there are opportunities a-plenty located within any curriculum anywhere, national or local. As long as there are educators with the 'professional energy' to provide and organise for choosing to become a living part of learning, children will act like the powerful learners they really are.

> *If educators can keep their collective professional eye on the big over-arching principle of* what matters to children… *they will be able to make absolutely certain that children do the right kind of learning.*
>
> *And because they can, they will.*   p.16

> *We do not see the key to meeting QCA's remit and developing a modern world class curriculum as producing more documents and sending them out to schools, or issuing yet more guidance and programmes.*
>
> *The key is to unleash the positive energy of the teaching profession and to allow it to focus on children's learning rather than the delivery of a set body of knowledge, allowing professional energy to take account of the 'big picture' of education and not get lost in details.*   Waters 2007:51 pp.7-8

A book for children

The Bee-man of Orn **by Frank R. Stockton**

The Bee-man spent all his days in the company of bees and was deeply content until he was told by the Junior Sorcerer that once he had been something else and had been transformed. The Bee-man, much disturbed by this news, set off to discover who or what he had been.

On his journey he met many and various dreadful people, none of whom he thought he could possibly have been, until he rescued a baby.

The Bee-man, convinced that he had once been a baby, persuaded the Junior Sorcerer to change him back to his original form. This child grew up to become, in the course of time, a bee-man.

> **Big ideas: conflict between destiny and choice**

A book for educators

In his own words **by Christian Schiller**

edited by Christopher Griffin-Beale

This book is a collection of speeches given by Christian Schiller between the years 1946 and 1975.

In the introduction Christopher Griffin-Beale writes

> *Every talk of Schiller, although only a fragment of his entire life's work, contains within it his entire philosophy of life and education – how children grow and how school should cherish their growth.*   p.viii

In Schiller's speech 'When a Boy or Girl is Creative' (1965), he emphasises the powerful part played by choice in the learning lives of children.

Review

These are the main themes of chapter C.

- When children choose they exercise their power to make decisions, find alternatives and trust their own judgements.
- This is vigorous exercise and educators have the capacity to provide and organise for it.
- Children need educators to be part of their nourishing diet, empowering them to make informed choices.

is for John Dewey:
experience and education

John Dewey (1859-1952), was internationally renowned for his writing on philosophy, psychology and liberal politics. But his most enduring influence is in the field of education. His 'laboratory school' at the University of Chicago, founded in 1896, was one of the first progressive schools, and his great work *Democracy and Education* (1916) is a comprehensive statement of his position that schools do wrong to separate mind from body, reason from emotion, thought from action, self from other, education from life.

In March 1938, at the venerable age of 79, Dewey gave a lecture in a banqueting hall in Atlantic City, New Jersey, which was rapturously received. Delegates were given complimentary copies of an expanded version of his speech on 'Experience and Education'; an immediate reprint was necessary, such was the demand for the text, which has since been through numerous editions; it is indeed a classic that has stood the test of time. Dewey's 'Experience and Education' is generally thought of as a penetrating analysis of the opposed ideals of traditional and progressive education, and is, as such, of great interest to historians of educational ideas. But it is also a text that has much to say to all practising educators of today, and tomorrow, in its brilliantly clear exposition of the necessary relation between the two key words of the title: experience and education.

All experience or some experiences?

His central message is forthright and direct: all education comes about through experience. But, and it is a very big but, this

> ...does not mean that all experiences are genuinely and equally educative... Some experiences are mis-educative.

From this bold opening, Dewey moves into a lively account of these mis-educative experiences and their devastating effects upon learners.

> It is a great mistake to suppose that the traditional schoolroom was not a place in which pupils had experiences... The proper line of attack is that the experiences that were had, by pupils and teachers alike, were largely of a wrong kind.
> 1963:26

Amongst other evils, students in the traditional schoolroom:

- *lost the impetus to learn*
- *came to associate books with dull drudgery*
- *were rendered callous to ideas*
- *learned ennui and boredom*
- *found what they learned completely foreign to their lives.*

Luckily for his present day readers, Dewey does not end his argument here; he is equally explicit about how educators can respond to the challenge he has faced them with: how to provide learners with experiences that are genuinely educative. He lays out three clear criteria, which, taken together, act as guiding principles on which all educators can draw.

The principle of continuity

Dewey argues that educators can understand the worth of an experience in terms of where it is heading.

> Every experience is a moving force. Its value can be judged only on the ground of what it moves toward and into.
> p.38

In other words, educators must provide experiences that are going somewhere, in terms of understanding: not dead-end, one-off experiences that land learners in a rut, but experiences that lead learners towards big ideas, and into difficult, complex, intriguing aspects of the world. And later he continues his argument,

> Unless a given experience leads out into a field previously unfamiliar, no problems arise, while problems are the stimulus to thinking.
> p.79

The problems children meet in their exploration of the world are, Dewey emphasises, an essential part of their nourishing diet as learners and thinkers.

The principle of desire

Dewey reminds educators that

> *...the greatest of all pedagogical fallacies is the notion that a person learns only the particular thing he is studying at the time... Much more important than the spelling lesson,*

[or, for today's educators, the synthetic phonics session] are the enduring attitudes that the children are learning at the very same time. And of these

> *...the most important attitude that can be formed is that of desire to go on learning.*   p.48

Learners who acquire this passionate commitment to their own learning are well-armed against the difficulties they may encounter; they are eager to meet what we call in chapter H, 'the promise of tomorrow'. These learners go to bed each night secure in the conviction that tomorrow's learning will be just as emotionally engaging and intellectually involving as today's has been.

The NOW principle

This criterion ensures that educators provide experiences that have meaning and relevance in the here-and-now, not merely in some unspecified future. Dewey emphasises the intensity of the present moment.

> *We always live at the time we live and not at some other time, and only by extracting at each present time the full meaning of each present experience are we prepared for doing the same thing in the future.*

And so the moral is clear.

> *Attentive care must be given to the conditions which give each present experience a worthwhile meaning.*   p.9

Compare and contrast: in a disturbing study of children aged between seven and ten plus, children who have mastered the beginning stages of reading, and who should be steadily becoming more proficient and experienced. Southgate et al (1981) questioned pupils, in individual interviews, about their attitudes to reading and why they thought children should learn to read. Only a tiny minority mentioned the pleasure or enjoyment of reading. *One seven year old boy

confirmed that he thought it useful for children to learn to read, but when he was asked why, his reply was disconcerting: *"Because then I can stop."* This young learner's experiences of reading have not met Dewey's criteria; his capacity for desire has been abused. The 'now' principle was not applied to his struggle with decoding and sounding out; he wants no more of it. The continuity of his learning has been threatened, his growth as a reader has been arrested. He has had the experience of being a learner of reading, he has tried out, at first hand, the activity of reading; but it was not enough.
Quite so, explains Dewey.

> *It is not enough to insist upon the necessity of experience, nor even of activity in experience. Everything depends upon the quality of the experience.*   p.27

Dewey's three criteria are powerful tools with which educators can work to provide the proper quality.

In a challenging commentary on this text of Dewey's, Philip Jackson, author of the classic study *Life in Classrooms* (1968), beautifully summarises Dewey's deep understanding of the organising concept of experience. When Dewey elaborates on his philosophy of education of, by and for experience, writes Jackson,

> *...he means that the goal of education, its ultimate payoff, is not higher scores on this or that test, nor is it increased feelings of self-esteem or the development of psychological powers of this or that kind, nor is it preparation for a future vocation. Instead, the true goal of education, Dewey wanted us to understand, is none other than richer and fuller experiencing, the ever-expanding capacity to appreciate more fully the living present.*   1998:138-9

> *Although Southgate's study was carried out a quarter of a century ago, it is worth emphasising that the same distressing scenario is being played out today. See, for example, Featherstone (2006), an edited collection of essays by literacy specialists about how and why children learn to read: for meaning, understanding and enjoyment.*

A book for children

The Hunter by Paul Geraghty

Jamina wants to be a hunter. Every day she plays at stalking, tracking and shooting, until the day when she finds a baby elephant with his mother lying dead nearby, a victim of hunters. Together Jamina and the little elephant search for another herd to adopt him. At night they sleep fearfully under the stars. Great is Jamina's joy when the baby is befriended by another herd and great is her relief when her own mother finds her.

Jamina's experiences in the real world have taught her much: she knows she no longer wants to be a hunter, she has learned to respect living creatures and to become self-reliant.

Dewey's principle of continuity, his emphasis on the worthwhile experience that leads learners to 'go somewhere, in terms of understanding', is clearly illustrated in this brave story.

Big ideas: grief
loneliness
fear
hope
security
understanding
through experience

A book for educators

Experimenting with the world: John Dewey and the Early Childhood Classroom

by Harriet K. Cuffaro

While there is no substitute for reading Dewey's own words, an American early years teacher, Harriet K. Cuffaro, has written an inspiring book that tells of her life long interest in Dewey's work, and her determination to apply his principles to her own practice. It includes some brilliant observations of sustained, complex, collaborative play in her own early years classroom; the extracts below are taken from the final chapter of her book.

With Dewey as guide, rather than embarking on a set itinerary or possessing a map to a promised land, we are offered an invitation to journey. We are told the terrain is changing, precarious and unstable... these conditions are to serve as catalysts, challenging opportunities to use our potential and capacity to grow, to expand our perspective and enrich experience... How much sustenance can be derived from Dewey's ideas and vision for the journey that is teaching?

...For myself, making sense of Dewey was a way of making sense of teaching, a way to question practice in the search for coherence and integrity in my work... Teaching is a way of being who we are and a place where in our actions we make manifest what we believe and value. Teaching is a way of rehearsing and trying identity, of creating and discovering self... Having Dewey enter my teaching was similar to listening to and trying to have a conversation with a reason-maker of teaching, to hear another story about teaching, and while listening to compare, contrast, question and try out reasons for my teaching.

...In the absence of absolutes and directives, Dewey asks the teacher to suspend the need for certainty, to accept the responsibility of freedom and choice, and to view self as capable of creating. This requires courage, initiative, a defined sense of purpose, intelligence, commitment and perspective, particularly the perspective that is born in hope and laughter. pp.98-100

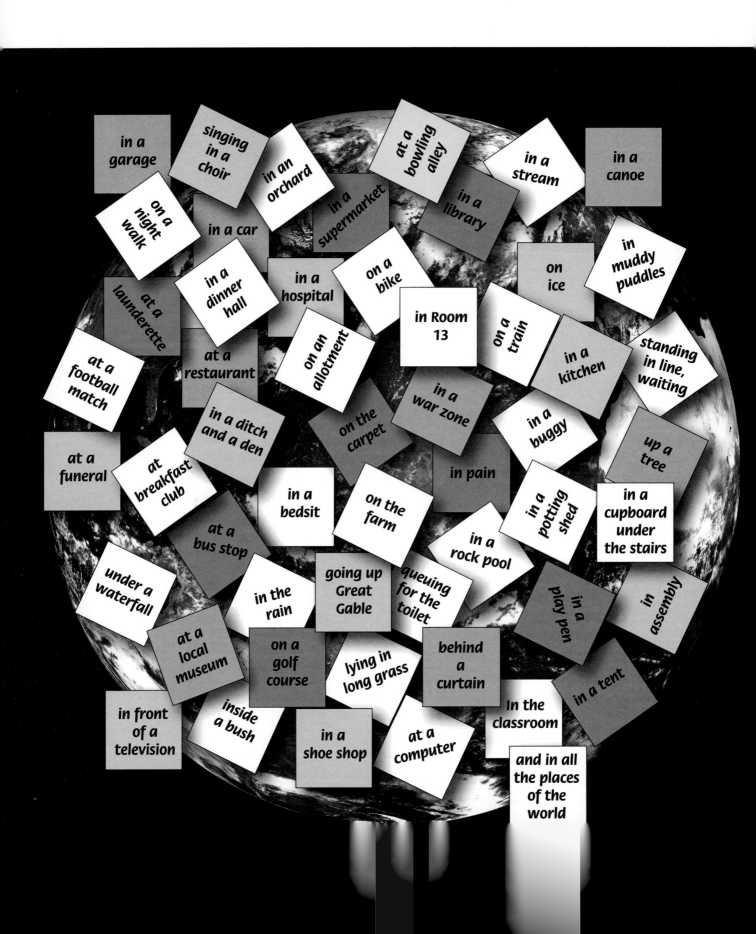

A book for children

Snail Trail

by Ruth Brown

This is the story of a journey seen as a snail's eye view of the world: up a hill, through a tunnel, into a forest, over a bridge…

Close to, it is difficult to understand the landscape. It isn't until the end of the journey that the map of everywhere can be seen, a silver trail through the entire world of the potting shed.

Big ideas: journey
travel
landscape
place
viewpoints
positions
panorama

A book for educators

The Genius of Play

by Sally Jenkinson

Not only is this one of the very best books about play ever written, it is also the book that above all others proves that play is the place where children learn most effectively.

"Remember", said the bad fairy, "Children learn everywhere, all the time."

What do learners do?
Learners *feel*

Mastery and helplessness

In a long series of ingenious problem solving experiments with young children, Carol Dweck (1999) and her colleagues have found two distinct patterns of learned behaviour, for which they use the terms 'mastery' and 'helplessness'. When children with a mastery orientation meet a difficult problem, they respond positively to the challenge; they show curiosity, perseverance and enjoyment. When children with a helpless orientation meet similar problems, they respond negatively; they exhibit anxiety, fear, self-doubt and tend to give up easily.

When they meet a challenge
MASTERY *learners feel something like this:*

"This is exciting!"
"I do enjoy something difficult."
"Something new... how interesting..."
"I think I can sort this out."
"It'll take time, but I'll stick at it."
"It doesn't matter if I can't do it right away."
"I`m sure I can sort it in the end."
"That was good fun! I knew I could do it."

These learners are using a theory about themselves which Professor Charles Desforges calls 'a red-hot learner theory'.

Whereas
HELPLESS *learners feel something like this:*

"Oh dear! I don't know what to do."
"I won't be able to do this."
"I'm not very good at this kind of thing."
"I don't want to get it wrong."
"How much longer will this go on for?"
"You see, I knew I'd get it wrong."
"There's no point in trying again."
"Can I stop now?"

These learners are using what Professor Charles Desforges calls 'a failure and a flop theory'.

Desforges 2006

Susan Isaacs

When Isaacs writes about children's learning, she uses a variety of terms from the domain of feeling. She writes of the 'strength and spontaneity of their wish to know and understand'; she constantly emphasises the interconnectedness of emotional and intellectual growth, of affect and cognition:

> *...the thirst for understanding springs from the child's deepest emotional needs... it is a veritable passion.*   1932:113

Her first biographer, Dorothy Gardner, who studied with her, and later became both colleague and friend, concludes that no-one who studied with Susan Isaacs would ever forget that:

> *...children cannot be emotionally satisfied unless they can also learn, nor really learn unless their emotional needs are met.*
> 1969:149

The role of the educator

🌿 **Whenever adults respond to children's feelings, they are faced with choices. Do they:**

deny, repress, distract, redirect ?   **OR**   **acknowledge, recognise, respect?**

What do children hear educators say?

"Don't be silly."	OR	"You are angry, aren't you?"
"You can't be frightened of this nice dog."	OR	"I should think you were frightened."
"Cheer up. It's not the end of the world."	OR	"No wonder you miss your little rabbit."
"Stop screaming."	OR	"I hate thunder too."
"No-one wants to hear you scream."	OR	"It does seem like a long time, doesn't it."
"That's not the way to get attention."	OR	"Hold on tight, I've got you safe."
"Here, let's blow your nose."	OR	"Let's see if we can sort this problem out together because it's important, isn't it."

🌿 **So how do educators respond when children doing learning talk about their feelings, about the challenges they meet, about themselves as learners? Are their feelings:**

dismissed as inappropriate?   **OR**   **respected and recognised?**

What do children hear educators say?

Appropriate feelings

In the *Practice Guidance for the Early Years Foundation Stage* (2007), the pages that describe Personal, Social and Emotional Development include a section on 'Self-confidence and Self-esteem'. One of the early learning goals in this section is as follows

 *Respond to significant experiences, showing a range of feelings **when appropriate**.* [emphasis added]

The problem is, who is to decide *what* feelings are appropriate?
And, equally, who is to decide *when* it is appropriate to show them?
The person doing the feeling? Or the nearby adult educator, who is not having that feeling?

Starting school

An article in *Nursery World* (1993) about starting 'at big school' with the title 'Is she READY?', includes a table showing 'Helpful skills for starting school.' Below this heading are three sub-headings:

- ten social skills
- ten independence skills
- ten emotional skills.

Two of these 'helpful' emotional skills are controversial, to say the least. The author recommends that four year old children starting at infant or primary school should be able to do things that many, many adults find difficult. These two items from the check list would be an interesting topic for discussion in any group of educators.

She should be able to:
1) Hold back tears when something goes wrong.
[...]
8) Accept a reprimand from an adult without becoming too distressed.

The Fear of Freedom

More than 60 years ago, the great sociologist and psychoanalyst Erich Fromm argued in his important book, *Fear of Freedom* (1942), that Western culture is characterised by pressures for conformity.

The suppression of spontaneous feelings, and thereby of the development of genuine individuality, starts very early.

He refers, in a footnote to this sentence, to a research report that shows that the attempts of three to five year old children to preserve their spontaneity give rise to the chief conflicts between these children and the authoritative adults who are closest to them.
Continuing his argument from early childhood into

Children sense the feelings of others

Angus, aged three, not only recognised the feelings of an adult, but also expressed his own feelings when he drew a picture which he called, 'My cross daddy'.

adult life, Fromm suggests that the discouragement and repression of feeling have serious consequences. Since all creative acts are inseparably linked with emotion, in accepting the standard of thinking and living without emotions, every individual is weakened,

...impoverished and flattened... Giving up spontaneity and individuality results in a thwarting of life. p.208

Feelings about learning: Tony and Patrick

A teacher asked her class of nine and ten year olds to draw pictures to illustrate what they felt about learning, encouraging them to do more than fall back on the conventional 'smiley-face' routine. The children's drawings were wonderfully varied, original, revealing. They drew a hurricane, a treasure chest, a charging rhinoceros, bags of gold, a blazing phoenix, a fiery dragon, a turbulent rocky river with a tiny swirling twig in it (labelled 'me'), a suspended noose, a person in the stocks, baby birds in a cosy nest. One girl drew three pictures, variously labelled:

'Here's me finding work a bit hard. (I'm tearing my hair out!)
But that's not how I feel.'
'Here's me sunbathing in Crete. (I'm SO BRILLIANT!)
But that's not how I feel.'
'I'm somewhere in the middle! And I'm HAPPY!'

Patrick made two drawings to show, first, how he had felt at the school he'd recently left, where the pressure for high SATS results was intense.

His second picture shows his response to his new school, where he was amazed by the comparative freedom he experienced.

Tony's drawing gave his teacher some concern. She asked him to say more about the threatening 100 ton weight. In reply, Tony pointed out that the weight was still suspended in the air; he felt that he was able to prevent it from crushing him completely, but that he was always aware of its presence. His teacher thanked him for telling her how he felt and promised to do all she could to prevent the weight from descending any further, indeed to try and lift Tony's sense of impending doom.

The drawings suggest that these two learners, for all their occasional feelings of alarm about what might happen to them, are, in fact, the kind of people whom Dweck labels 'mastery learners'. They are determined, resilient and ultimately optimistic.

Janusz Korczak (1878 1942) 'King of Children'

Janusz Korczak was a Polish, and more significantly, Jewish doctor who introduced progressively run orphanages, designed as just and harmonious communities, into Poland, in the years leading up to the second world war.

His inspiring life, and tragic death, in the gas chambers of Treblinka, alongside his orphans, is movingly documented by Betty Jay Lifton in her biography *King of Children* (1989). As an advocate for children, Korczak often spoke of the need for a Declaration of Children's Rights, long before any such document was officially drawn up. His own declaration was left uncompleted at the time of his death, but, drawing on key writings, Lifton has compiled a list of the rights Korczak considered most essential.

Among these we find

> *The child has the right to respect for his grief. 'Even though it be for the loss of a pebble.'*
> p.356

Adam's story

Adam, aged seven, was soon to move to a new school, away from his friends, security and life as he knew it. He expressed his feelings in this poem.

> *Sometimes I just have to cry,*
> *I don't know why,*
> *There is nothing really very wrong.*
> *Perhaps I could pop a couple of*
> *Balloons or watch cartoons,*
> *Or sit and tinker with my toys,*
> *But I'm feeling sad,*
> *I don't know why,*
> *And all I do is sit and cry.*

In *Understanding Children's Play* (2001) Jennie Lindon describes how children play out distress and anxiety.

> *Children's play may be a means of coping with overwhelming feelings, but the play re-enactment does not necessarily resolve the distress... Milder less traumatic stress is sometimes worked out through play. Children may use play in preference to talking with parents or other carers. Alternatively, children may use play alongside talking about the incident or requesting that familiar adults talk around what happened.* p.35

Feelings about a new baby sister

Daisy was born when Lucy was five. Naturally this arrival unsettled Lucy; although she was helpful, loving and attentive to her new baby sister, her play showed that she felt displaced and wanted to re-establish her place in the family.

When her uncle came round to see the new baby, she played Swingball with him. The game took its regular form to start with - post in the middle, rope attached to post, ball attached to rope, two players each with a bat.

Then Lucy added variations, gradually encroaching on the territory of her uncle, until a pattern developed; she ran to the spot her uncle had left when he sprang for the ball and jumped into it with both feet announcing loudly, "I AM HERE AND THIS IS ME! I AM HERE! I AM HERE!" forcing her uncle permanently out of his place. Then she added, "I am the Princess and I am here." As her uncle left for home, she thrust a hastily drawn picture into his hand, proclaiming, "It's the Princess Family: the King, the Queen and me the Princess."

A book for children

Frog

by Susan Cooper

Through this story children can empathise with the feelings of learners as they struggle with new skills. They encounter the feelings of failure and hurt caused by unkindness, but also care and delight in achievement.

Little Joe couldn't swim. All his family could, and they laughed at Joe's attempts, insensitive to his hurt and feeling of failure. Then a frog came to the swimming pool and Joe watched it swim. But a swimming pool was not a good place for a frog. The sides were slippery and steep. It could not escape its watery prison. Joe carefully helped the frog back to its own habitat and then turned his attention to swimming. With the help of the frog, Joe could do it.

Big ideas: *care*
gentleness
success and failure

A book for educators

Self Esteem and Successful Early Learning

by Rosie Roberts

This book for educators is enticingly structured around stories from the life of an imaginary (and completely real) family with two children under three, who are described living, learning, growing, feeling, finding their place in society. The children's stories centre around the themes of self-concept and self-esteem.

Every story is followed by analysis and commentary, in which Roberts makes it crystal clear that living with children and their powerful feelings is both challenging and complicated. She sensitively argues the need for balance,

> *...understanding the child's point of view as well as our own; accepting the normality of bad feeling as well as good ones; finding ways of accepting*
> *feelings at the same time as setting limits for behaviour.* p.xv

Roberts' thoughtful commentaries are short and direct, but offer readers so much; they are intensely supportive, resolutely practical and firmly grounded in carefully selected research studies of young children.

Review

These are the main themes of chapter F.

- The process of learning is always emotional as well as intellectual; no-one can do worthwhile learning with a cold heart.
- 'Children cannot be emotionally satisfied unless they can also learn, nor really learn unless their emotional needs are met.'
- Children spontaneously express their feelings, especially in their play – unless adults prevent or discourage them.
- Play is one of the ways in which children learn to understand themselves, their identity and their relationships with others.
- Learners' feelings are not all positive: some children feel fear, anxiety and frustration as part of their learning. It is important to acknowledge and respond to these genuine feelings, so that all children can feel the excitement and confidence of mastery learners.

What do learners do?
Learners need a generous environment

The Malting House School

Writing in 1930, a few years after she had left the Malting House, Susan Isaacs used the phrase 'a generous environment' to describe the experimental school that she had directed from 1924–7. When she was appointed as its principal she was 39 years old, with a bunch of qualifications: she was a qualified infant teacher, with a Masters degree in Psychology; she was also a qualified psychoanalyst, one of the first women in England to qualify and then practise in what was then a very new discipline. For the last few years before she went to the Malting House, she had been teaching in a teachers' training college in the North of England.

The school was the brain child of an eccentric millionaire, Geoffrey Pyke, who wanted his son David, then four years old, to have an education different from any other in the history of childhood, an education free from any kind of emotional stress or compulsion, free from fear, anxiety and pressure, based on scientific enquiry and self discovery. No such school existed so he was obliged to invent it, and happily for everyone he hired Susan Isaacs to lead it and develop his educational ideals.

When the school opened it was barely a school at all: just ten children, aged from a little under three to five years old. By 1929, when it closed, there were 20 children, and the age range had extended to include children from three to ten years old. The Malting House was a big rambling family house, standing in an extensive garden, right by the river in Cambridge.

One kind of generosity

The children did their learning both indoors and out of doors in the large garden. There were two lawns, an orchard of fruit trees, real bricks for building and a space for bonfires. Animals were plentiful: there were at different times, mice, rabbits, guinea pigs, two cats, a tortoise and a dog, hens and their chicks, a grass snake, lizards and salamanders, silk worms, a wormery, a fresh water aquarium and thousands of tadpoles. There was a sand-pit with a water tap, metres and metres of hose-pipe, lots of ladders and a climbing frame. On top of all this there was a tool shed with an invitingly low, sloping roof that every child naturally wanted to climb. Although the school was rumoured to have no rules, there was a rule about this roof; by present day standards it was a very unusual one, but effective none the less. The rule at the Malting House was 'only one child on the roof at a time.'

Indoors the provision was equally generous; there was one large hall with a raised gallery and a piano, and four smaller rooms, one set up as a science laboratory, with every kind of authentic equipment – flasks, test tubes, Bunsen burners – with which the children did magnificent experiments. They had microscopes and dissecting instruments; they did a great deal of biology and what Isaacs calls 'looking inside animals.' Another of the small rooms was for carpentry, staffed by a part-time carpenter; the equipment there, besides saws, hammers, nails, planes, drills and other authentic tools, included a full-size working lathe. And everything else was provided for on the same lavish scale: everything the children could possibly need for drawing, painting, modelling and construction. There was a plentiful supply of textiles for sewing of all kinds: one hot summer all the children made themselves little muslin shirts. There was a library of books and a typewriter... in short, it was a treasure chest of an environment.

Another kind of generosity

But that was only one of the ways in which this environment was generous: there are two others. One of these is in the big ideas the children were studying; Isaacs and the other teachers made copious notes of everything the children said and did, which form the basis of Isaac's book, *Intellectual Growth in Young Children* (1930). So although the school closed nearly 80 years ago, there is a clear and vivid record of the thinking that went on there. Isaacs describes what the children were interested in and what they studied; they studied how plants and animals work, how they live and die: they studied life and death. They studied gravity and evaporation, diversity and growth, the causes of things, the functions of things, the origin of things. They studied heat and light and combustion. They were especially interested in burning - and what the Bunsen burners would and would not burn. They studied steam and boiling water. They studied mechanical principles, they studied cause and effect and how machines work – pulleys and balances, bicycles and tricycles.

And a third

These two kinds of generosity and abundance, huge quantities of 'stuff' for children to handle, and the abundance of big ideas, which the children encountered every day of their lives, are not the end of the story.

There was a third kind of generosity: an abundance of time for all this thinking and doing. As a result the children were extraordinarily active, more active, more curious, more creative, more exploratory, more inventive than children in a less generous environment could ever be.

They wasted no time in the meaningless school rituals of registers and forming lines, or waiting to hear about the tasks assigned to them; they simply dived into the richness of the environment that had been provided and proceeded to make the very best of it.

The way we live now

It goes without saying that there are many, many striking differences between the conditions in which Susan Isaacs worked and the contexts of today. We are not suggesting that educators should attempt to re-create the Malting House in all its details. But we are suggesting that lessons can be learned from the Malting House story to apply in schools and settings today. In particular, educators could learn to adopt and adapt the concept of the generous environment: the generous provision of material resources, the generous provision of time and space, and the abundance of big ideas, the conceptual richness of the children's thinking and doing.

Whatever the framework, local or national within which educators operate, today, there is always scope to make choices in the best interests of children; furthermore, the criterion of generosity is a powerful tool with which educators can evaluate the effectiveness of their provision. This argument is developed more fully in the introduction.

A book for children

Roxaboxen

by Alice McLerran

Rocks, boxes, sticks and stones, broken bottles and discarded pram wheels are all found at the town rubbish dump, known by the children who play there as Roxaboxen. It provides a rich resource for play, a generous environment in which the children explore their roles as leaders, followers, bandits and home builders. The children never forget their play and recall it years later with love and enthusiasm.

Big ideas: **community**
making collections
resourcefulness
memory
roles and responsibilities

A book for educators

Little Men **by Louisa May Alcott**

Louisa May Alcott and her three sisters, all well known to generations of readers as the four March girls in *Little Women* (1868), were educated at home by their eccentric father, Bronson Alcott. An early progressive, Bronson founded a succession of experimental schools, all of which failed to secure enough pupils, and the last of which, the Temple School in Boston, collapsed in 1837, when Bronson shockingly admitted a black child in line with his position on abolition.

But Bronson's unconventional methods have survived, transformed into the fictional school Plumfield, most fully described in *Little Men*. Plumfield is an integrated, co-educational, inclusive school, managed by the wild tomboy Jo March in her new role as the motherly Mrs. Bhaer, wife of the German immigrant Professor Bhaer: 'a happy,

homelike place', Jo calls the school at the end of *Good Wives*.

The children spend very little time in the school room; far more important in their lives are the garden, the orchard, their dens, the trees they climb, their band, their story telling, their menagerie, their museum and the stream they regularly fall into.

Little Men can be read as an account of the good life, for adults and children, being lived in a good society, where children largely educate one another. They do so through their turbulent and passionate relationships, as well as through their play, their shared imaginative explorations of the world, and their intrepid physical explorations of their generous environment.

Review
These are the main themes of chapter G.

- Learners thrive in an environment that is rich in materials, animals, people and all manner of things that they can get close to, handle, explore, examine and think deeply about.
- Learners thrive when they encounter big ideas that are relevant and meaningful to them.
- Learners thrive when they are offered an abundance of time and space in which to learn.
- Learners thrive when educators respond generously to their interests, concerns and anxieties – to *what matters to children*.
- The concept of generosity is a useful criterion for educators to use in evaluating every aspect of their provision.

What do learners do?
Learners hope

A ray of sunshine

"Monica [9 months] is my ray of sunshine. When she wakes she bounces into each day. I think if she could talk she'd say, '*What have you got for me today? Come on Mum, it's a great world, isn't it? Let me at it. What's the adventure for today?*'"

Wise words

Wise words from moral philosopher Mary Warnock (1986) in an essay on 'The education of the emotions'.

It seems to me that education is particularly fitted to encourage hope... To feel competent, able to act, able to change or control things, or even to create them, these are all aspects of feeling hope... To find that today you can begin to do something you could not do yesterday, is to begin to hope. For someone to wake up in the morning, thinking 'Good: I can go on with it,' whatever 'it' is, this I suppose must be the chief goal of education.   p.183

Witches and fairies

In a wonderful passage in Iona Opie's *The People in the Playground* (1993) two junior school girls come flying down the steps into the playground at playtime. One says to the other "Going on with witches and fairies, right?" The classroom is left far behind as the children are absorbed into the far more immediate world of make believe. Effortlessly they re-enter the story they are creating together in their play, the story that has been waiting for them through the long morning lessons. Their capacity to pick up the narrative, and 'go on with it', in Warnock's phrase, is characteristic of learners who are truly committed to 'whatever 'it' is'. This capacity for commitment and continuity will serve learners well in any kind of learning, but only when the experiences, tasks and activities that are offered to them deserve such a whole-hearted commitment of the mind and will.

Getting to the heart of the matter

Observations of teaching and learning made in a mixed class of nine to eleven year old children, in an inner city primary school, standing in a neglected and seriously disadvantaged area of a major industrial city are reported in *Learning Without Limits*, Hart et al (2004),

The class teacher, Narinder sees learning as a three-dimensional process. Alongside her responsibility for the intellectual work of meaning making, forging understanding, she places the imperative of attending to the social dimension of learning: 'Learning to resolve conflict, tolerate each other, respect and be respected... these are all the foundations of learning on which acquiring academic knowledge can take place.

Equally important is the emotional component of learning; she explains 'You have to get to the heart of something for them to feel the emotion of it, for them to respond to it.' Expanding on this principle, she argues

The root of their lives is, you know, fighting, violence, burglaries, break-ins, broken homes. Their whole lives are turmoil, and for them to come to school, they have got to see some purpose in it, they have got to have some success, and they have got to enjoy school to come in next day, to see what was the pleasure of it.   p.90

It is clear that Narinder's classroom is 'particularly fitted to encourage hope', as Warnock advocates.

At the end of each day in school, Narinder's class meet together as a whole learning community to review their learning. But they do not only look back at the events of the day, at the connections they have made, and the understandings they have reached; Narinder invites them to look ahead, to their future learning, to what we might call the promise of tomorrow,

...a promise Narinder seems to give her pupils after each day's learning, assuring them that the purposes for which they worked today will still be alive, worthwhile and engaging, on the following day.   p.98

A book for children

Mrs Frisby and the Rats of Nimh

by Robert C. O'Brien

Mrs Frisby, a field mouse and mother of a large and hopeful family, has to move her home before the plough destroys it. She does this every spring, but this year is different, because her son Timothy is too ill to move. With great determination, ingenuity, perseverance and the unexpected help of a group of rats, Mrs Frisby works against the clock to keep her family safe. She never gives up hope.

Big ideas: *family*
friends and enemies
safety and danger
survival in difficult times
triumph over adversity

A book for educators

What Is and What Might Be **by Edmund Holmes**

When Edmond Holmes retired in 1910, he had been an inspector of schools, including a stint as Chief Inspector, for 35 years. He waited until he retired to speak his mind in this remarkable book, which appeared in 1911.

As the title suggests, Holmes treats two themes: in 'What Is' he describes the current disgraceful state of elementary education as he sees it, which is 'in the highest degree anti-educational'. In 'What Might Be' he describes a real alternative, one particular school, which he calls Utopia, but was in fact a small village school in Sussex. He uses this genuine school, and its Froebel trained teacher, to illustrate his conviction that education could be a nourishing and enriching force in the lives of children. The moral he draws from the stark contrasts he depicts is that there are always choices to be made, by all educators, in the interests of every child they encounter.

This is one of the oldest books that we have selected, but its message is crucially contemporary. In all his writing* Holmes remains doggedly optimistic that one day, when educators make a bolder use of their freedom, by making more appropriate choices, they will be able to create the environment that living, growing, learning children need and deserve. In his autobiography, *In Quest of an Ideal* (1920) he sketches the key features of such an environment,

Trust first and then freedom. Freedom, because without freedom the child could not learn to do anything for himself. Trust, because without trust, one could not begin to set him free. p.120-1

*Some of Holmes' ideas about children's learning are more fully described in chapter O.

Review

These are the main themes of chapter H.

- The capacity to hope, to wake up in the morning committed to 'going on with it', whatever 'it' may be, is central to the internal lives of engaged, active learners.
- Educators do not have to wait for feelings of hope to arise spontaneously in the hearts of children; they can act to increase the commitment that every child brings to the learning that lies ahead, 'the promise of tomorrow'.

What do learners do?
Learners *imagine*

The centre of thinking

Imagination is not some desirable but dispensable frill... it is the heart of any truly educational experience: it is not something split off from 'the basics' or disciplined thought or rational enquiry, but is the quality that can give them life and meaning; it is not something belonging properly to the arts, but is central to all areas of the curriculum; it is not something to ornament our recreational hours, but is the hard pragmatic centre of all effective human thinking.

Egan and Nadaner 1988:ix

There is always some measure of adventure in the meeting of mind and universe, and this adventure is... imagination. Dewey 1958:267

When children imagine

To imagine requires the ability and experience to recreate in the mind some thing, some one or some place. When children imagine they can travel to other worlds of place and time, meet other people, real or fictional, past or present; they can be different:

grown up	*compassionate*
brave	*kind*
afraid	*beautiful*
hungry	*ugly*
adventurous	*fierce*
courageous	*threatening*
excited	*dominant*
apprehensive	*a leader*
sympathetic	*triumphant*

Children can make sense of their own experiences through play; they can shape, change, recreate, extend, distort, enlarge, exaggerate and realise them in new forms.

With imagination...

With imagination children can ask questions that might ultimately make a mark on the world:

What would happen if...?

How would it work if...?

Does it need to be like this...?

I wonder why...?

With imagination...

With imagination children can respond to worlds created by others: the worlds of dance, music, literature and art.

Stories and poems and the singing words that made them, lightened my darkness, were a joy and comfort to me all through my early childhood.

Morpurgo 2007:57

With imagination...

With imagination children can create their own worlds of dance, music, literature and art, transforming experience into new realities.

Carl, aged seven, wrote the following poem having watched a duckling emerge from its shell:

A small, alive, damp, stuck fast chick
Cracks and explodes on a new world
And it`s straight out for a swim.

With imagination...

Scientists, engineers or designers can make changes to the world by taking imaginative leaps into projected possibilities.

Imagine being someone else

Very young children enjoy stepping into the shoes of others: there was shock on a father's face when his 18 month old son, Daniel called out unexpectedly in a tiny squeaky voice from behind a teddy twice his size, "*Tea, sugar, me.*"

He had started on his travels in the landscape of the imagination.

Imagine a space ship

In her inspiring book, *The Genius of Play* (2001) Sally Jenkinson describes how imagination is the force through which children move away from the known, the rational, the here and now and venture forth into the unknown, engaging with the possibility of what might be.

> *Our imagination fires our will forces and we act to change the world. In play, children are also practising changing the world. Combining something seen with the senses, with the imagination of a new context, they change the world – just as they see adults do around them.*
>
> *Some boys in an indoor up-turned table-boat needed a radar. A black metal music stand was spied and instantly appropriated to function as a sky scanner in a new and imaginative setting. Few men and no women have set foot on the moon, yet thousands and millions of children have been there, in a variety of self assembled play spacecraft, or in invisible flights of swift and soaring imagination.*
> p.59

Solving real life challenges: imagine a door that doesn't slam

In a class of five and six year olds a door blew shut on a windy day, trapping a child's fingers. The children were very concerned and sympathetic, resolving to prevent this from happening again. Their teacher invited them to invent something to serve as a doorstop. Wood and tools were always available, the children knew how to use them and so they designed, made and tested a range of doorstops, the most efficient of which was used on a daily basis.

Food for imagination

Educators can provide an environment that is generous in first hand experiences, opportunities and challenges, including:

- ❧ **things both natural and made to handle and wonder about**

- ❧ **scientists, artists, dancers, musicians and poets to talk to and work with**

- ❧ **places to visit: woods, beaches, streams, caves, castles, ditches, ruined buildings, old buildings, building sites, art galleries, museums and theatres**

- ❧ **being out and about: at night, in the wind, in the snow, in the mist, in the rain**

- ❧ **opportunities for imaginative play**

- ❧ **stories, poetry and music**

- ❧ **dances to watch and join in**

- ❧ **intriguing questions to explore**

- ❧ **tools and materials for making art and music**

- ❧ **tools and materials for designing and building**

- ❧ **tools and materials for writing and illustrating.**

Living in the imagination

> *We hear much nowadays about the cultivation of the child's 'imagination'. Then we undo much of our own talk and work by a belief that the imagination is some special part of the child that finds its satisfaction in some one particular direction generally speaking, that of the unreal and make believe, of the myth and made-up story. Why are we so hard of heart and so slow to believe? The imagination is the medium in which the child lives.*
> Dewey 1889:61

Imagination and experience

Imagine a hospital

As an advisory teacher I once worked with the staff of a primary school to help them develop imaginative role-play throughout the school. After some inset sessions with teachers, support staff and parent governors, the educators agreed to prepare role-play areas in full consultation with children. The nursery class set up a hospital because one child was an expert on all things 'hospital', having recently been admitted. Another class expert came forward, with experience of visiting an uncle in hospital. Children also interrogated the teaching assistant whose arm was in a plaster cast. They used their experience and imagination to make sense of hospitals and find out what would happen if robbers, dogs, or sick babies turned up. Their stories were captured on film, written down and told back to the players and their classmates, who received them with delight.

Imagine a windmill

In the same school, educators of the eight and nine year olds set up a magnificent windmill role-play area but when I arrived I found the area was no more than a pile of broken boxes and lifeless sails. The educator moaned, "Don't ask me about it, just don't ask. It was awful." She described what had happened, "Whenever they went into the windmill they just played Power Rangers. We'd set up a windmill because it linked with our science work on wind power. But it was a nightmare, so I told them to break it all up."

I listened sympathetically, but was having some trouble imagining what life in a windmill might be like, never having visited a working mill, so I asked, "What happens in a windmill?" The answer came back swiftly and clipped, "Oh, I don't know.", followed by a look of stunned realisation.

Children will play to the limits of their knowledge and that includes the limits of their knowledge about life in windmills. In order to imagine and play at 'life in a windmill' the players have to have something from the windmill world on which to base their windmill play.

Imagine a bird

A book for children

The Great Good Thing

by Roderick Townley

This book explores the relation between the real world and the world of the imagination. Where does one end and the other begin?

A reader, Claire, opens a story book to find that the main character, Princess Sylvie, is eager to escape the confines of the story and explore Claire's world of dreams and imagination. They have many adventures together, until a fearful day when the book is burnt, and Sylvie cannot return home. She and her family can only live in the memories of those who know the story.

Claire is responsible for keeping the story alive.

> **Big ideas:** where reality begins and ends

A book for educators

Primary Understanding

by Kieran Egan

This is a book to read slowly, taking one's time. Only a slow reading can do justice to the complexity of Kieran Egan's thinking and his masterly progression from the general principles that might guide educators' choices in framing a curriculum for early primary education, to the particular forms such a curriculum might take: the specifics of what is to be taught and how.

At the centre of Egan's argument is his particular understanding of *what matters to children*: those parts of their mental lives powered by imagination and fantasy. Misled by their mis-reading of Dewey, Egan claims, educators have focussed their attention on

> *...the mundane and practical world in which [children] live. What has been lost is the ability to see that world as the child sees it, transfigured by fantasy.* p.204

Egan's insights into the vivid, imaginative, intellectual lives of children, his account of *what learners do*, lead him to make clear and controversial recommendations for educators.

> *Our early curriculum then, is to be made up of important content that is rich in meaning for children. Its meaning will derive from its being articulated on concepts they know from their experience – love/hate, fear/ security, good/bad, courage/cowardice and so on – and our curriculum concern will be to get at what is of importance to our social and cultural lives.* p.199

Review

These are the main themes of chapter 1.

- Imagination is the hard centre of human thinking.
- Children imagine in all areas of their thinking: in play, in problem solving, in representing their understanding of the world.
- When children imagine they build on all previous experience.
- When children imagine they make sense of big ideas.
- All educators have the capacity to provide for the growth of children's imaginative powers.

What do learners do?
Learners do joined-up learning

Everybody loves a list

Perhaps there is an innate human propensity to tidy up the chaos and confusion of the turning world: there must be some reason why, sooner or later, prescriptions and descriptions of what constitutes worthwhile learning are reduced to a list.

Some lists of the elements of worthwhile learning are simple, others complex; some short, others too long to be committed to memory. All of them reflect the pressures and priorities of the day; none of them take account of the inescapable fact that children's hearts and minds are not ruled out into sections and sub-sections that correspond to any list, past, present or to come. Wherever they are in the world, children do joined up learning.

Diderot's list

In the eighteenth century, the radical atheist philosopher, Diderot, and a group of his associates, drew up the syllabus for the great *Encyclopédie*, eventually published (with many passages excised), in 35 volumes between 1751 and 1765. The sale of the book was repeatedly and officially banned by the Catholic authorities, but this magnificent work, the first of its kind in the Western world, could not be suppressed. Diderot's project was to catalogue all of humanity's great achievements, to bring order and system to all of secular society's accumulated knowledge and wisdom. Diderot's list was simplicity itself: all that was known was to be organised under just three headings:

Memory ❧ Reason ❧ Imagination

What a bold approach: to list the three chief intellectual powers of humankind as a way of ordering the achievements of the entire species, living and dead.

Susan Isaacs' list

Fast forward to the early twentieth century, and another way of categorising human impulses, desires and interests. In *The Children We Teach* (1932), a short summary of what she had learned from the children (from under three to eleven years old) whom she had so attentively observed at the Malting House, Susan Isaacs lists the three spontaneous activities that filled their days:

- ❧ *the love of movement and perfecting bodily skills*
- ❧ *the interest in actual things and events, the discovery of the world without*
- ❧ *the delight in make-believe, the expression of the world within.*

Another bold approach: a powerfully comprehensive list of *what learners do.*

The title page of the great Encyclopédie

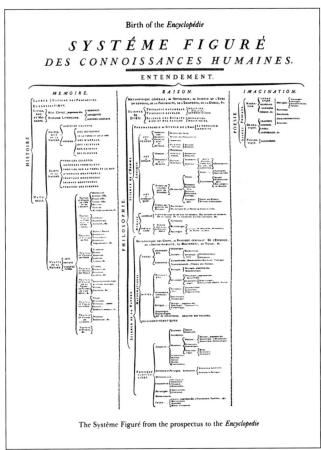

The title page of the great Encyclopédie from Furbank (1992)

Lists from the 1970s

During this decade, the Schools Council funded a number of curriculum development projects; some of them are worth revisiting in this brief historical survey of memorable lists.

The *Communication Skills in Early Childhood* project, for example, led by Joan Tough, at the University of Leeds, offered educators a framework for listening to and fostering children's spoken language. Drawing on the first hand observations and analysis of M.A.K. Halliday, and her own empirical studies, Tough described seven 'Uses of Language', seven different things that children do in their talk:

> *Self-maintaining*
> *Directing*
> *Reporting (on both present and past experiences)*
> *Reasoning*
> *Predicting*
> *Projecting*
> *Imagining*   Tough 1976

The *Communication Skills in Early Childhood* project encouraged educators to listen attentively to children's spoken language, recognising the different purposes for which they used their talk.

Its sister project, the S*tructuring of Play in the Infant/First School*, focussed on 12 aspects of play and development; thousands of teachers and other educators all over England and Wales used these 12 categories to observe children's play and learning:

Emotional	*Manipulative*
Social	*Problem-solving*
Language	*Motivation*
Mathematical	*Drama/role-play*
Scientific	*Concentration*
Physical	*Curiosity*

Manning and Sharp 1977

Both of these projects supported educators in seeing more clearly the richness of *what learners do.*

The *Progress in Learning Science* project referred to 24 elements of children's learning in science, grouped under three headings - concepts, skills and attitudes:

Concepts	**Skills**	**Attitudes**
Cause and effect	*Observing*	*Curiosity*
Classification	*Problem-solving*	*Originality*
Weight	*Raising questions*	*Co-operation*
Length	*Exploring*	*Perseverance*
Area	*Finding patterns*	*Open-mindedness*
Volume	*Communicating*	*Self-criticism*
Time	*verbally*	*Responsibility*
Life cycle	*non-verbally*	*Independence*
	Applying learning	

Harlen 1977

It is interesting that this list of concepts explicitly defines examples of what the **What Matters to Children** team describe as big ideas, the important concepts with which children make sense of their perceptions of the world.

The two lists, of skills and attitudes, can be seen as variations and extensions of the themes of this book: the things that learners do and how they do them.

From the US, during the same period, came the High/Scope Cognitively Oriented Curriculum, developed on Piagetian principles. Echoing Isaacs' list of spontaneous activities, the High/Scope list is organised around a set of *Key Experiences:* what children actually do:

Language • Representation • Classification • Seriation • Number • Space • Time • Movement • Social/emotional

Hohmann et al 1979

In High/Scope schools and classrooms detailed anecdotal records were (and still are) kept of every child's learning in these nine areas of experience.

An official version

In the mid 1980s, a series of booklets was issued by Her Majesty's Inspectorate (HMI), disrespectfully known as the raspberry-ripple series, because of their lurid pink covers. Of these, the one that has left the most enduring mark on English educational history is *The curriculum from 5-16* (DES 1985), in which nine areas of learning and experience were proposed for the entire statutory age range.

Nine areas of learning and experience
aesthetic and creative
human and social
linguistic and literary
mathematical
moral
physical
scientific
spiritual
technological.

It is interesting to see how the use of alphabetical order in this list seems to give high priority to areas of the curriculum that later, after the introduction of the National Curriculum in 1988, became less important relative to the core subjects of English, maths and science.

In addition, HMI proposed

Four elements of learning
(knowledge,concepts, skills and attitudes)

Five characteristics of the curriculum
(breadth,balance, relevance, differentiation, progression and continuity).

In a second edition of this booklet, (in 1989, i.e. post National Curriculum), the teaching profession was urged to use these lists as an analytical framework to complement the National Curriculum and also to take account of

Nine essential issues
(environmental education
health education
information technology
political education
education in economic understanding
preparation for the world of work
careers education
equal opportunities for girls and boys
ethnic minority groups).

[Perhaps there should be a line of comment here? But what to say? Besides 'Phew!!']

A learning story (c.1966) from a secondary school

In 1966, Philip Toogood, a radical and progressive teacher, was working as Head of History in a purpose-built, house-based, community comprehensive school in Cumberland. In his professional autobiography, *The Head's Tale* (1984), he describes his early efforts to understand the boundaries of his single subject department and its resources: 'Was a book on 'Water' with its chapter on water-mills a history book? There was a water-mill at the end of Egremont High Street. Was it geography, science or history?'

His history department was soon broadened to become a Humanities Department, taking up the whole top floor of the Science Block. And later, the whole teaching approach in this new department changed, transforming the previous traditional system of routines, bells, individual lessons and 'box' classrooms. A chance observation gives a flavour of the new approach.

> *During one of our second year 'Man and Technology' modules, I came across a boy who had opted for doing an individual project, seeming to do nothing as he gazed out of the window, elbows resolutely dug into the window-sill in a glazed trance which I mistook for 'inattention' as I approached him. He turned to me almost without recognition and spoke of his amazement at the phenomenon of weight, mass, size, atomic structure of matter etc. Then he said, in a more light-hearted mood, 'It's a funny school this one – here up in Humanities we are spending our time talking about Physics and downstairs yesterday in my physics lesson, I was definitely doing history!*
>
> 1984:61

This student seems to have grasped the very big idea that big ideas cannot be tidily contained in sealed and separate lesson periods.

Learning without lists

After leaving the Cumberland school, Toogood went on thinking, trying to make more complete sense of these issues. By the end of *The Head's Tale*, his professional autobiography, he has arrived at some kind of synthesis, and is ready to offer a summary of his new understanding of knowledge, which he sees as an intensely personal process of acquisition, energised by two breathtakingly simple questions:

Who am I?
This question is asked by students engaged in dialogue with themselves about the nature of their own being.

What is there?
This is a question about material surroundings, about the total environment of time, and beyond time, about people in their surroundings and beyond.

Thinking about these two questions, says Toogood, leads to knowledge. And in this sense

> *...knowledge is arrived at as a process of becoming oneself, in an adventure of learning. It is never complete.*

The need to join things up

Since 1988, more lists have arrived in England, for example from *Birth to Three Matters*, the *Early Years Foundation Stage* and its six areas of learning, the *Every Child Matters* agenda. These are too familiar to many educators to need reproducing here.

All these lists, however interesting or important their individual elements, suffer from a common flaw. By breaking down the complex whole that is education into smaller and, possibly, more manageable parts, they invite the charge of fragmentation and reductionism. What should and must be big, becomes little; what should be connected is taken apart. Professor Charles Desforges calls this process 'dismembering'. In a paper given in 1992, and so relating to the lists of the day, the currently prevailing model, he uses vivid, indeed bloody, imagery.

> *This so-called analysis is no more than butchery. A corpus of knowledge representing concepts, skills and attitudes, is no more use than a heap of limbs. The question is, how does it work when it is together?*
> Desforges 1992:16

What educators need is not a heap of dismembered limbs, but a joined-up understanding of what living learners do, a coherent, articulated, working model of children's powers – to think, to do, to feel, to understand, to represent and express – powers that can be exercised in any and every 'area' of learning or curriculum.

Joined-up learning to make a worthwhile whole

> *In this book we focus on what learners actually **do**, the verbs of learning, active children belonging, choosing, feeling and representing and so on. In every chapter we consider a single verb of learning, but each of these, stitched together with play, links with other verbs to make a joined-up, worthwhile whole.*

A book for children*

The Water Hole by Graeme Base

This book joins many ideas together in the context of a simple counting book. At first glance on page one, there is only one rhino drinking at a water hole. But on closer inspection there are more animals hidden in the exquisite illustrations, awaiting discovery. As the pages turn, the landscape changes, and new animals gather at the water hole. The list of animals increases as more arrive, the water in the pool diminishes, until it is empty. No water, no life. But then it rains. The world and the water hole fill with water and the animals return.

Big ideas: the richness of variety
increase-decrease
extinction
no water-no life
the earth in crisis

*or for an irresistible book about lists, go at once to
Frog and Toad Together by Arnold Lobel

A book for educators

Te Whãriki: the early childhood curriculum Ministry of Education, New Zealand

This is the first national curriculum document for the early childhood sector in New Zealand; six years in the making, it is the result of widespread consultation with specialist reference groups and educators from the rich variety of early childhood settings across the country. It is a powerfully inclusive, bilingual document, integrating care and education for children from birth to school entry age (five years).

The Maori word *whãriki*, which means a traditional woven mat, is used as a central metaphor for the curriculum that each individual setting will weave from the agreed principles, strands and goals defined in the document:

Four principles
Empowerment
Holistic development
Family and community
Relationships

Five strands
Well-being
Belonging
Contribution
Exploration
Communication

The text elaborates each of the principles and strands in practical, positive and supportive detail; but none of the headings given above is to be considered, or 'delivered', in isolation. The weaving metaphor is constantly emphasised: the curriculum is woven from the non-negotiable principles and the essential strands of learning and development. This is a truly joined-up approach, which still allows for diversity; different programmes, philosophies, structures and environments are not strait-jacketed into uniformity, but encouraged to develop their own distinctive patterns.

Review

These are the main themes of chapter J.

- Children's learning is divided into sections by adults, for many purposes, some of them entirely admirable and illuminating. But children do not do learning in separate sections; they do joined-up learning.
- Children exercise and strengthen their powers as learners in any and every engaging and challenging encounter with the world.
- Looking at lists of learning, old and new, demonstrates that there is a variety of ways in which others have chosen to think about children's learning.
- But it is also important for educators to think about how their awareness of the elements of these lists can contribute to their understanding of learning as a whole.

choos

What do learners do?
Children know more than adults think they do

Professor Piaget visits Susan Isaacs' school in Cambridge

During a visit of Professor Piaget to the school, he had been remarking to me that he had found that the appreciation of mechanical causality does not normally occur until eight or nine years of age, and that with regard to bicycles, for instance, children of that age rarely have any understanding of the function of the pedals. In drawing the bicycle, they will put the pedals in, but not show their connection with the machine. He asked how our children stood in this respect. At that moment, Dan, (aged 5 years 9 months) happened to be sitting on a tricycle in the garden, back-pedalling. I went to him and said, "The tricycle is not moving forward, is it?" "Of course not, when I'm back-pedalling", he said. "Well," I asked, "how does it go forward when it does?" "Oh, well", he replied, "your feet press the pedals, that turns the crank round, and the cranks turn that round" (pointing to the cogwheel), "and that makes the chain go round, and the chain turns the hub round, and then the wheels go round – and there you are!"

Isaacs 1930:33-34

Wouldn't it have been wonderful to have witnessed Piaget's discomfiture? But still more wonderful is the achievement of Dan, the quality of his thinking, his mastery of language. Look at his confident use of precise words about each part of the tricycle and the way he fits them all together to produce a completely logical, accurate explanation. Dan so clearly understands the 'big idea' that Piaget calls 'mechanical causality' – or, more simply, the concept of cause and effect. Dan also understands another big idea, the principle that the size and shape of things, the form of things, is closely related to their function, so that each different part of the tricycle is related to its individual different function, which all culminate in the movement of the wheels – which go round – as Dan observes. And there you are!

A river of stars: knowing the power of story openings

Educators in a nursery were concerned about a four year old boy, Simon. Like the boy Paley describes, 'who would be a helicopter', Simon preferred to drive round the room in an imaginary car for most of the day; other children appeared anxious around him, he wasn't interested in the books on offer at nursery, he appeared not to be engaged with what went on around him, preferring to be in his own world.

The educators set about observing him more closely.

One day two girls were playing together with a story box containing various figures, brought to life as they played. Some contents had been discarded, including a strand of sparkling, star-studded blue tinsel. Simon drove past the girls in his imaginary car. He stopped and watched them, making gentle engine noises. He turned off the engine and continued to watch silently. He opened the car door, stepped out, shut and locked it with a click of his mouth and the twist of a key. He moved closer and picked up the strand of starry tinsel. The girls carried on with their play. Simon held the tinsel above their story box and said, "This is a river of stars that has fallen from the sky. There can be no story till the light shines." He went on holding up the tinsel as the girls played, to light up their story and ensure that it continued. After that, every time the starry tinsel appeared in any story box, children held it up and began their play with Simon's irresistible story opener: "This is a river of stars that has fallen from the sky. There can be no story till the light shines".

These extraordinary words show Simon's great knowledge of stories and how they work. The educators confessed that they were humbled by Simon knowing far more about the world of literacy and making stories than they had given him credit for. His capacity to entice his listeners with his magical words made Simon a story hero.

Tom's learning story: a headteacher remembers

Tom, aged six had always been regarded as a difficult child to teach, as indeed he was, due to two distinct allergic conditions from which he suffered a good deal: he was 'allergic' to both instruction and authority. These afflictions meant that although he took part in many classroom activities, it was always on his terms and conditions, and never as the result of a teacher's directive.

Tom was soon to leave infant school for a junior school with a highly formal and rigid approach. Unfortunately for his prospects there, Tom was not yet reading and writing independently. Indeed he had barely ever been known to pick up a pencil, though he loved to spend time with books, but always alone, far from the teacher's pedagogic gaze.

One morning I had a long conversation with Tom about a model he was making with Lego, a massive spaceship of military design, bristling with rockets. We talked about the problem of military might, the threat of nuclear destruction and the prospect of global disarmament. Tom concluded the discussion with a fine summary: "And that's why the world is a mess." My reply was, I hope, encouraging: "Why Tom, that would be a fine title for a book. You write it, I'll publish it, and we'll split the profits." At which point I took my leave.

Some hours later, I noticed Tom at the door of my office. I was not welcoming, assuming he was in trouble yet again. Tom, in his turn, was offended and indignant. He reminded me of our conversation: "I have come to write that book!" I changed my tune at once and supplied him with a clean exercise book. He sat down at a table, I entered the title of the book on the contents page, and was dismissed back to my own work. This is the completed contents page, which he wrote some weeks later.

Why the world
is
a mess

Contents

1 a ha 8 isdoms
2 is radish
ε posn pepol
4 pon pepol
5 hodes
6 vondels
r mrs
thaεhep

At last the great work was complete, and Tom set off around the school to read his book to anyone who would listen. As his teachers should have predicted long before, Tom went on to flourish as both an accomplished writer and reader.

A commentary on Tom's learning

If Tom's achievement is measured against any kind of standard for effective literacy, it is easy to identify his deficits. But the achievement remains. Tom's first written text is a coherent book, nine chapters long, fired with a sense of social justice, and driven by his inner convictions, not by any curriculum framework. There are no standards by which to measure Tom's achievement; it is unique, unpredictable, magnificent. He may not know much about the formal aspects of literacy, spelling and punctuation. But he does know how:

- to persist and persevere
- to organise his thinking and his arguments
- to compare and contrast
- to recognise the big ideas in our complex society
- to strive for social justice
- to project his thoughts into the lives of others
- to care for his environment
- to reason and persuade

...and more, much more.

1 and 8 is bombs; 2 is rubbish; 3 posh people; 4 poor people; 5 robbers; 6 vandals; 7 Mrs Thatcher

48

What do children know about reading?

A fascinating study of children learning to read in the US by Bruno Bettelheim and Karen Zelan (1982) shows how children know a great deal more about the kinds of texts they are reading than they are given credit for.

The story of their research starts with the familiar observation that many children teach themselves to read

> *...being children who have acquired a love of reading by being read to. The child who enjoys being read to learns to love books.* p.8

Bettelheim and Zelan contrast these children, 'who learn to read from texts that fascinate them', with children who learn to read only in school, by

> *...being drilled in skills of decoding and word recognition from texts devoid of meaningful content that are demeaning to the child's intelligence.* p.10

Bettelheim and Zelan talked to these children, the ones who had had the diet of these 'demeaning' graded primers.

> *Without exception, the children complained about how stupid the stories in their basic readers had been, and said how much they hated having to read them. With venom they spoke of 'all those sweet little kids in the stories', furious that the stories assumed they were so simple-minded as to believe that children were like that... When asked why they had not expressed their opinions about these readers before, the answer was that nobody was interested in their true thoughts on this matter; everybody wanted only to hear that they liked the stories. One mature [nine year old] girl remarked 'In none of the stories does anyone ever say his true opinion, so how could we?'* p.14-16

Bettelheim and Zelan implicitly invite all educators to reconsider their judgements about what reluctant readers may be reluctant to do – and why. Why *should* children engage with texts that are unworthy of them, without worthwhile content, or emotional integrity? The principle of *what matters to children* is relevant here; Bettelheim's and Zelan's work makes it very clear that children are experts in applying this principle for themselves, even if their teachers have lost sight of it.

Wise words from Loris Malaguzzi

(The first pedagogical director of the municipal schools in Reggio Emilia)

'Children are always ready to shake the tree of knowledge.'

Children's knowledge of world events

On September 12, 2001, after the twin towers terrorist attack, staff groups in nurseries and schools all over the world were unsure of how to deal with the events of the previous day. One staff group in a nursery met early to work out a strategy before the children arrived. They agreed that their approach would be to take the lead from children. They would wait to see how much children knew about it and how they reacted and observe what they chose to play with. They would listen to children talking as they played and respond honestly and directly to any questions.

Jagdip, aged three and a half, was the first child to come bursting through the nursery doors; he went straight to the blocks, where he remained for much of the day. Like some children in similar settings everywhere, he was preoccupied with building two tall towers, flying planes around them to knock them down and then rebuilding them all over again.

At the end of the day Jagdip's mother collected him as usual. But half an hour later she returned, very irate, to talk to staff. She demanded to know why Jagdip had been told about the terrorist attack and how he had come to know so much about it. She accused the staff of teaching fear, of failing to protect her child from, as she put it, "the evil of the world". She described the lengths to which she had gone to keep details from Jagdip, turning off the television and radio so that he did not hear news reports, constantly diverting his attention and keeping him occupied. She informed the stunned staff that she had completely protected him from the terrible news; to prove it she described the journey to the nursery that morning, when Jagdip appeared innocent of all knowledge of the terrorist attack. She kissed him goodbye at the door through which he happily disappeared.

That morning he had to make sense of both the terrorist attack and his mother's protection.

The First R
How Children Learn Race and Racism

Carla, a three year old child, is preparing herself for resting time. She picks up her cot and starts to move it to the other side of the classroom. A teacher asks what she is doing. "I need to move this," explains Carla. "Why?" asks the teacher. "Because I can't sleep next to a nigger," Carla says, pointing to Nicole, a four year old Black child on a cot nearby. "Niggers are stinky. I can't sleep next to one." Stunned, the teacher, who is white, tells Carla to move her cot back and not to use 'hurting words.' Carla looks amused but complies.

This shocking story, set in an ethnically diverse day care centre in the US, appears on the first page of an alarming book, the title of which stands at the head of this section. The book convincingly shows that young children are more than capable of learning things that adults wish they would not, and that they know some things adults do not want to believe they know.

The authors, one of whom made this observation of Carla, go on to analyse her knowledge and understanding of the world in which she is living and learning.

Like most of the children we observed, Carla is not the unsophisticated, innocent child of many adult imaginations. This three year old knows how to use racial material, such as the hurtful epithet, which she has learned from other sources. But she is not just imitating what she might have heard in some other social setting. She applies this particular bit of racial knowledge to a distinctive and personal interactive encounter. The range of concepts she has linked together are remarkable. She has not acted indiscriminately, using an ugly name only to foster a reaction in the other child. Instead, Carla uses 'nigger' to explain and justify her action to... the teacher. This shows a level of forethought. She has considered what a 'nigger' is, to whom the appellation applies, and why such a label is useful in explaining her behaviour to an adult. This is not the thoughtless blunder of a sleepy child.

Van Ausdale and Feagin 2001:1

Van Ausdale and Feagin carefully spell out their starting point, which is a confident rejection of assumptions that children's thinking and understanding are immature and inadequate, that children are simply incapable of grasping complex ideas such as racial identities.

Most adults refuse to accept that young children would make knowing use of the ugliness inherent in racist epithets, emotions and behaviour. Most parents do not believe that small children can understand what such language implies. When children do employ racial or ethnic terminology they are assumed to be mimicking some other adult's behaviours... Most important, racist talk and behaviour is usually dismissed by adults as being of little consequence and is not taken seriously till children are older.

p.3

The authors of *The First R* see children differently. They see them as competent learners 'actually doing life'. Another example starkly illustrates their claims.

During playtime, Renee (4, white) pulls Lingmai (3, Asian) and Jocelyn (4.5, white) across the playground in a wagon. Eventually Renee drops the handle, and Lingmai jumps from the wagon and picks up the handle. As Lingmai begins to pull, Renee admonishes her, "No, No. You can't pull this wagon. Only white Americans can pull this wagon".

p.37

Alarming as this observation is, and there are plenty more, the authors do not write out of despair. They are honest about the pain suffered by the first author Debra Van Ausdale, who carried out the observations.

Watching little children indulge in hateful rhetoric and hurtful interracial activity was the hardest thing Debi had ever done, and there were many occasions when she wanted nothing more than to leave the field to cry.

p.vii

But they steadfastly maintain an optimistic stance; they are committed to finding ways of working with what they have learned about children. The final chapter, 'What Can Be Done?' emphasises that the more educators know about what children know and understand, the more effective they will be in challenging and eliminating racist behaviour.

> *If we are ever to know fully what race and racism mean in the larger society, we must understand what they mean to children. We need to know more about how children 'do racism,' why they do it, when they do it, and with whom they do it. And we need to know about these things as early as possible in children's lives.*
> p.214

A book for children

How Tom Beat Captain Najork and his Hired Sportsmen

by Russell Hoban

Tom is a boy who fools around. His Aunt Fidgit Wonkham-Strong calls it 'play' and despises it. She summons Captain Najork and his hired sportsmen to teach Tom a lesson, but Tom's experiences of fooling around, playing with the real world, have taught him a thing or two. He knows more than the adults think he knows. He takes them on and beats them hollow.

Big ideas: artful proficiency
competition
fooling around with words
gamesmanship
ingenuity
romance

A book for educators

Children's Minds

by Margaret Donaldson

This highly valued, ground-breaking book has changed the way educators think about how young children learn.

Writing in the 1970s, Donaldson responds to the problem of falling standards amongst school leavers, many of whom finish schooling illiterate, innumerate and unfit for work. She questions how so many adolescents have become disillusioned, isolated, with such an acute sense of personal failure; she asks whether school experience is really the best it can be for children. She considers who might be failing: children or their teachers?

Donaldson looks to the early years of schooling for a solution, considering what can be learned from educators' approaches to young enthusiastic learners, who are skilled users of language and sophisticated thinkers. She famously calls into question the laboratory situations on which Piaget based his theories, in particular rejecting his claim that pre-school children are limited in their ability to 'decentre', or appreciate someone else's point of view. She shows that young children can successfully engage with all kinds of demanding intellectual tasks when these are embedded in real life, meaningful situations, linked to their understanding, experience and growing powers.

Review

These are the main themes of chapter K

- In looking at children's learning, there are always choices to be made: whether to look at what children do not know, or have not learned; or whether to look at what they do know and have already learned.
- If children have learned things they have not been taught, or are experts in fields unfamiliar to their educators, it is possible to underestimate their learning, sometimes with damaging consequences.
- Some kinds of learning (especially, perhaps, the learning that matters most to children) are not best understood by using the measures with which educators are most familiar (levels, standards, test performances).
- Some aspects of society are undeniably inequitable, unjust and violent, about which many children inevitably know a good deal. Knowing about these unwelcome and disturbing kinds of learning will enable educators to work more effectively for a better world.

What do learners do?
Learners need libraries of books

Oh, I love the library. You can go there to get books. I go there. My Grandma goes there. Everyone goes there. I saw my teacher there once. It's a nice place. It's quiet. I like that it's quiet. Everyone who likes books should go to the library. I've got books at home and I play libraries. A library is just books and books and books and if you like books, go there. I love my library and my books.

Emily, aged five

We don't need lists of rights or wrongs, tables of do's or don'ts: we need books, time and silence. 'Thou shalt not' is soon forgotten, but 'Once upon a time' lasts forever.

Pullman 1996

Making sense of the world: what matters to children

To open a book is to open a treasure chest and is accompanied by the same anticipation. First there is the cover that invites children inside. The title provides clues to the content, and the illustrations tempt children to enter the world within. Once inside, children find nourishing food: factual knowledge of how the world works and knowledge of the human spirit. Every book enlarges their experience, their feeling, their understanding, and helps them build their own world maps.

In story books children meet choices between right and wrong and encounter good and bad behaviours. They respond instinctively in support of heroes and hope for the defeat of villains.

But life is more complex than these simple opposites: right and wrong, good and bad. In story books children meet other points of view, where traditional roles are reversed and there is more than one kind of acceptable behaviour. Things may not always be as they first appear: story books can challenge assumptions and prejudices.

Stories in books reflect the realities of being in the world; they tell it how it is. Children relate to the experiences and feelings of the characters. Every book acknowledges and expands the children's range of experience.

Readers meet big ideas

Books are good to do thinking with, as children encounter the big ideas that are the sub-text of every story. In story books children meet tales of friendship, enemies, justice, retribution, fear, courage, grief and survival that can be springboards for discussion or promote private reflection.

Educators can provide a rich range of books for children to share with them and leave them to enjoy on their own. But it is vital that educators are aware of the power of what they are dealing with. It is important to read a book before sharing it with a group of children, to be aware of the issues and the big ideas it contains. To embark on a story without knowing its potentially sensitive content is to enter uncharted terrain. Nowhere is this more important than in the choice of books that touch children's deepest feelings.

Issues that were once taboo in children's literature, such as death, loss, warfare and discrimination are now the subject of many beautifully written and illustrated books.

The story books we describe at the end of each chapter will make children laugh, cry, wonder, puzzle, empathise or rouse their anger. Books such as these are powerful tools for feeling as well as thinking.

A book for all reasons

There are many other kinds of books apart form story books. A book can be a mine of information, a route to further discovery, confirmation of ideas, an eye opening source of wonder. While some children may love to pore over their parents' Haynes car manual, some will be fascinated by detailed illustrations of the human body found in family health guides. Others will be enthralled by a dictionary, a thesaurus or a telephone directory.

But there are also many books written for children that open their minds to the wonders of the world. There are biographies of artists, scientists, explorers, inventors and discoverers, books to invite reflection on the state of the planet, to explain how the world works, books that explore culture, place and time. These bring children face to face with the richness and variety of the world. Providing children have had plentiful experiences of the real world, these books will extend the big ideas they have already met. More than that, these books will introduce children to fresh ideas, leading them down new paths in their search for understanding.

There are books for all reasons: a bumper harvest just waiting for young reapers. Or should it be readers?

Readers create themselves: becoming a reader

> *Authors do not create readers, they create books. Readers create themselves.*
>
> *Mark 2003*

To become readers children need access to books: books in the library, in the book corner in their setting, on their own personal library shelves at home. To be the owner of a library of books that are personal choices, built up over time, that reflect changing interests and ongoing pursuits, or to have the opportunity to select a book from a book shelf in the setting or the local library to develop those interests, is to belong to the world wide group of people who are dedicated readers.

As children become readers they learn that when they open a book they may find inside something that will delight, engage, inform and change their thinking. It is not necessary to be able to decode the text to be a reader. A year old baby bringing a book to share with an adult is becoming a reader as much as a child who queues for the latest *Harry Potter* novel. They both anticipate the magic that unfolds from the very first page.

A book for children

I Believe in Unicorns

by Michael Morpurgo

In this story Tomas, who hates school and has no belief in himself as a learner, gradually becomes drawn towards the irresistible power of stories while reluctantly visiting the local library. As he listens to the stories told there, Tomas finds that he has a voice and things to say; the stories reflect his own yearnings, hopes and fears. He comes to realise that books are central to his life.

Big ideas: **having your own voice**

the transforming power of imagination

the essential place of books in people's lives

A library for children

Apart from the 'bookend' chapters A and Z, every chapter ends with synopses of two books. One is a **children's book** and the other a **book for educators**, each chosen for its particular relevance. Our collection of children's books, a wonderful library, is shown on the shelves below.

Children's Books

A

B — Grandfather's Journey   Allen Say

C — The Bee-man of Orn   Frank R. Stockton

D — The Hunter   Paul Geraghty

E — Snail Trail   Ruth Brown

F — FROG   Susan Cooper

G — ROXABOXEN   Alice McLerran

H — Mrs Frisby and the Rats of Nimh   Robert C. O'Brien

I — The Great Good Thing   Roderick Townley

J — The Water Hole   Graeme Base

K — How Tom beat Captain Najork and his Hired Sportsmen   Russell Hoban

L — I Believe in Unicorns   Michael Morpurgo

M — The Mysteries of Harris Burdick   Chris van Allsburg

N — Daddy's Lullaby   Tony Bradman

O — The Crane Wife   Odds Bodkin and Gennady Spirin

P — Fossil Girl   Catherine Brighton

Q — Why do the stars come out at night?   Annalena McAfee

R — The Legend of the Indian Paintbrush   Tomie dePaola

S — Imagine a Day   Ron Gonsalves

T — The Time of the Lion   Caroline Pitcher

U — Plum   Tony Mitton

V — Frederick   Leo Lionni

W — The Sleeping Sword   Michael Morpurgo

X — THE GARDEN   DYAN SHELDON

Y — Hooray for Diffendoofer Day!   Dr Seuss

Z

54

Books for educators

Educators need libraries too, collections of books that help them to understand the extraordinary richness of children's learning. In every chapter we have selected a book for educators, but these are not enough for a library of books. We supplement these with more books on the shelves below. They are a selection of three different kinds:

Old but not obsolete

Books that have stood the test of time; they have had an enduring impact on generations of readers.

Books about children

What better way to learn about children than to be put in the hands of an author and taken inside the world of a child?

New classics

Recent books that we predict will inform or challenge current thinking.

Review

These are the main themes of chapter L.

- ❦ Books are essential to children in their quest to make sense of the world.
- ❦ Every book contains its own big ideas but a library of books gives children opportunities to make personal responses, make connections, consider points of view, research, exchange ideas, resolve conflicting ideas and compare.
- ❦ Educators are responsible for providing books in abundance, ensuring there are books for all reasons.
- ❦ Educators need libraries too, collections of books that help them to understand the richness of children's learning.

What do learners do?
Learners *make meaning*

The Reggio view: children making meaning

Carlina Rinaldi, former director of the municipal early childhood centres in Reggio Emilia, for children from birth to six, writes eloquently of children's search for meaning.

I believe that some of the most important questions we have to ask ourselves as teachers, but also as educators in general and as adults are these:

🍃 *How can we help children find the meaning of what they do and what they experience?*

🍃 *How can we respond to their search for the meaning of life itself?*

🍃 *How can we respond to their constant questions, their 'whys' and 'hows', their search for that which we like to think of as not only the meaning of things but the meaning of life itself, a search that begins from the moment of birth, from the child's first silent 'why'?*

These are central questions.

...It is a difficult search, especially for today's children, who have so many different points of reference in their daily lives: the experience of the family, television, the places of socialisation. Young children make enormous efforts to put together all these often disconnected fragments, which they encounter not just over a lifetime but even in the span of a single day. And in these efforts children are sometimes left alone, by their families and also schools. But they continue their search just the same, stubbornly, tirelessly, making mistakes, and often doing it alone, but they persevere...

This search for life and for the self is born with the child, and this is why we talk about a child who is competent and strong, engaged in this search toward life, toward others, toward the relations between self and life. A child therefore, who is no longer considered to be fragile, suffering, incapable... Ours is a different idea and attitude toward the young child, who we see as active and who, along with us, searches everyday to understand something, to draw out a meaning, to grasp a piece of life.

2006:111-2

The Meaning Makers

The Bristol study 'Language at Home and School', directed by Gordon Wells, was a major longitudinal project, which included following a small group of children from shortly after their first birthday until their last year in primary school. The most accessible, and exciting, account of the findings of this study is to be found in Gordon Wells' book *The Meaning Makers: Children Learning Language and Using Language to Learn* (1987).

The bulk of the book is taken up with transcriptions of the children's talk, at home and at school, with their writing, as they move through primary school, and with Wells' brilliant analysis of what is happening in their learning. But there is also plenty for teachers and other educators to think about in terms of their responsibilities for the powerful learners that Wells describes. Two examples follow:

[on the well-known precept 'start where the child is'] All too often this is interpreted in practice to mean 'Administer a test or some other form of assessment in order to decide which ability group to place the child in, or which reading primer or worksheet to give him or her.' But this is not discovering where the child is – what his or her mental model of the world is like or what his or her current needs and interests are... Really to discover where a child is and, hence, how we can most helpfully contribute to his or her further learning, it is necessary to listen to what he or she has to say – to try to understand the world as he or she sees it. p.118

From observations outside school, we know that children are innately predisposed to make sense of their experience, to pose problems for themselves, and actively to search for and achieve solutions. There is every reason to believe, therefore, that given the opportunity, they will continue to bring these characteristics to bear inside the school as well, provided that the tasks they engage in are ones that they have been able to make their own. p.120

The final paragraph of the book, *The Meaning Makers*, is a masterly summary of all that has gone before.

Conclusion
We are the meaning makers – every one of us: children, parents and teachers. To try to make sense, to construct stories, to share them with others in speech and in writing is an essential part of being human. For those of us who are more knowledgeable and more mature – parents and teachers – the responsibility is clear: to interact with those in our care in such a way as to foster and enrich their meaning making.   p.222

Dean revisits his nursery class

Dean's educators were worried about him: two weeks after starting school, aged four, they reported, "He doesn't really talk at all…he has never answered the register, volunteered any information, or replied to a single question." The school Dean attended was part of a research project into children perceived to be having language problems in school. The project researcher, Jacqui Cousins, spent time observing Dean, whom she found in the playground, peering through a fence at his old nursery classroom. After playtime she and Dean went to visit the nursery, accompanied by a tape recorder.

The nursery children had gone out for a walk so Jacqui and Dean had the place to themselves. Dean was soon attracted to an indoor pond that the nursery staff had constructed in a corner of the room, and that Dean remembered well. A long conversation took place beside the pond. Here is a short extract.

Dean: *That thing there's a frog. See, look up the rock. He can eat… all they eat. Mrs. J. stuck a bit of meat in a string, like a knotted bit, and dangle it in the water. They got big mouths eating that meat, an't they? .Look, what that thing? [pointing and putting his face near the water] That a fish?*

J.C.:   *Think so… can't really see it for all the weeds.*

Dean: *Fish got eye flaps?*

J.C.:   *Got what Dean?*

Dean: *Eye flaps…like mine? [pointing to his eyelids]*

J.C.:   *[laughing] Eyelids! I like your name- 'eyeflaps'. I don't really know. What made you ask that question, Dean?*

Dean: *That fish sleep. Look, him fast asleep but he never shut him eyes.*

J.C.:   *Why do you think he's asleep? He might just be watching. His eyes are open.*

Dean: *No, no… him sleep 'cos, 'cos fishy not move him tail. He stop still in the weeds.*

Hughes 1989:154

This is a remarkable demonstration of Dean's capacity to make meaning, to puzzle away, out loud, about an interesting phenomenon: in this case a motionless fish in the weeds, who may or may not be asleep. To resolve this problem one way or the other, Dean needs to know whether the fish has eyelids. He invents his own fine word, 'eyeflaps' to try and extract the information he needs from Jacqui, and masterfully explains his hypothesis. This story illustrates that, as Gordon Wells so firmly maintains, all children are

…innately predisposed to make sense of their experience, to pose problems for themselves, and actively to search for and achieve solutions.

1987:120

'All children' includes children like Dean, whose powers as thinkers and users of spoken language have not yet been recognised by their educators.

Gerry's learning story, told by his classteacher

The hero of this story is a five year old boy called Gerry, the youngest of an unusually large family of six children. And a wonderful thing had just happened in that family, which I'll explain in a moment.

One morning, all the children were outdoors in the playground, and Gerry came rushing up to me with something precious clutched in the palm of his hand. He was so excited he could hardly speak; he showed me a wood-louse and said, when he could get the words out: "Miss, Miss, this wood-louse is having babies!!!!" Now everyone in the school knew that Gerry was interested in babies, because that was the most important idea in his life. Until last week, Gerry had been the baby brother of his family. Now, however he had a new-born sister – a beautiful baby of his own.

Just the same, I thought he was deluding himself. I thought he was wrong. Everyone knows that wood-lice don't have babies. Wood-lice aren't furry mammals, who give milk and have babies. Wood-lice are crustacea, they are like crabs and lobsters and prawns. None of those have babies: they lay eggs. We all did biology at school; I know that, you know that. Or do we? Back in the classroom, we put the wood-louse under the binocular microscope; the children went and fetched the box of magnifying glasses – and it seems that Gerry is right! We can all see the tiny baby wood-lice swarming across the parent's underbelly, from where they seemed to have crawled out. Up to the school library to look at the biology books, and check that we are not imagining things: diagrams and detailed textual explanations tell us that the female wood-louse is more like a kangaroo than a crab in this respect; it has a brood-pouch on each of its four back legs, where the eggs stay after they are hatched until they are strong enough to crawl out, just as Gerry had so brilliantly observed.

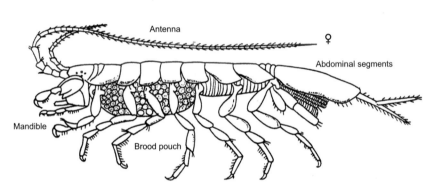

This is a fine example of one child's desire to explore for himself the natural world, and in doing so, to make sense of it, on his own terms and conditions, pursuing his personal concerns and interests. It shows how this child's desire to understand, and his intellectual energy, made him more aware of the world, more attentive to what is in it and how it works, than his teacher with all her fine qualifications in biology.

Five year old Gerry wanted the world to make sense, so he was acting as a genuine scientist, observing acutely, comparing, and above all making connections. He was asking himself something like this: "If my own mother, who I've known all my life, can suddenly have a tiny baby, whatever next? Can everything have babies? Does everything have babies? Even wood-lice?" And his great discovery is a splendid piece of learning, because it matters to him. It is spontaneous enquiry, for a real, personal purpose. His observation makes real human sense to him. He is doing worthwhile learning, taking vigorous exercise.

The baby in the snow

Katie aged three, talked to herself as she played. She had recently heard a news report of a baby in Canada, mysteriously disappearing from her bed at night to be found many miles away seemingly dead in the snow. No-one knew how the baby had got there. The report focussed on the miraculous recovery of the baby, which confounded doctors.

As Katie played she moved around the nursery, gathering resources while playing being on a train, a recent event in her life. As she played she talked to herself, telling a story and saying the words of a mother, "There was a baby and a mummy. It was night time. Mummy had lost her baby. She said, "Baby, baby, where are you my baby? Baby, baby… I have lost you my baby.""

[Katie rushed around searching, then lay down to sleep, resuming her talk.]

"The baby was asleep. She woke up. She climbed onto a pussy cat. The cat took her to the train station. She climbed onto the train and the train went a long, long, long way away."

[Katie set off around the nursery.]

"It went to the snow. The baby got off the train. The baby climbed onto a doggie. The doggie took the baby to the land of snow. The baby fell asleep."

[Katie lay down to sleep, then announced.]

"The Mummy has found the baby. The ambulance man put the baby in a special blanket and the baby woke up. Mummy was happy and she loved the baby."

In her play Katie drew on recent experience and her knowledge of the world of books to make meaning. She called on a world where cats and dogs talk, babies ride on animals to go on long journeys and lost children are found.

Katie's story was highly valued by children and adults. It was told to groups in the nursery, with her permission, on many occasions. Other children used her play resources (a soft toy cat, dog, baby and blanket) to play, 'The Lost Baby and the Snow'. White sheets were used to extend large role-play in a snowy land.

Making sense of a science test

One section of a standard assessment task (SAT) in science included two items designed to measure six and seven year old children's understanding of forces. The first item showed a drink can standing on a table and instructed children to 'Draw yourself using a force to make the can move. Write what is happening.' The anonymous hero or heroine of this learning story duly complied and wrote, 'I am pulling the can to make it come from one side of the table to another side.' But when the child read through the second instruction, the response was less conventionally compliant.

Draw yourself using a force to change the shape of the can. Write what is happening.

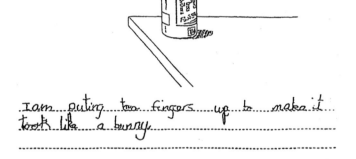

I am puting two fingers up to make it look like a bunny.

This response is not out and out rebellion; the task has been completed, but only in a delightfully unexpected way. Is it an inappropriate or incorrect response? Only if educators always assume that there is only one answer to a question, or that the understanding children bring to the problems they are set can be specified in advance. In this splendidly deviant response there is evidence of a child's fine mind at work, enlivening an undemanding task, a low-level challenge, with a flash of street-wise wit.

A book for children

The Mysteries of Harris Burdick **by Chris van Allsburg**

This is a book of mysterious pictures. Their mystery lies not only in the way they were discovered, but in the pictures themselves and the intriguing caption beside each one. It is a book with which children can make their own meanings from both the image and the captivating phrase.

Big ideas: *authorship*
infinite possibilities
mystery
origins
the power of words
and images

A book for educators

The Idiot Teacher
by Gerard Holmes

This book tells the story of the achievements of Teddy O'Neil, who trained as a teacher in 1911 and became the headteacher of an elementary school in the Lancashire village of Prestolee in 1918, where he remained until his retirement in 1963. It was a school of intensely progressive ideals, made intensely practical and realistic, where everything the children did made human sense to them.

The final chapter presents 'The Proverbs of Teddy O'Neil,' slogans that epitomise his approach to education. Two of these proverbs will introduce the man and the school, the vision and the reality.

> THE PROBLEM OF EDUCATION
> IS THE IDIOT TEACHER:
>
> • FOR WHOM NO PROBLEM EXISTS
> WHO EXPECTS CHILDREN TO DO WHAT HE HIMSELF
> CAN'T - LEARN
> WHO CAN ONLY DO WHAT HE HAS DONE
> WHOSE QUALIFICATION IS THAT HE HAS PASSED HIS
> EXAMS
> WHO IS REPETITIVE AND UNCREATIVE
> WHO HAS NEVER REALLY LIVED
> WHO HAS A BUS TO CATCH
> THE BETTER TEACHER MISSES THE BUS

> A SCHOOL SHOULD BE:
>
> A PLACE FOR LECTURES AND TEACHING
> A WORKSHOP FOR YOUNG AND OLD-OF BOTH SEXES
> A DEN OF HOBBIES AND INDOOR GAMES
> A STUDIO FOR DRAWING, PAINTING AND PLASTICS
> A MUSIC STUDIO
> • A HALL FOR SONG AND DANCE
> AN EDUCATIONAL SHOP-WINDOW
> A REFERENCE LIBRARY
> A PICTURE GALLERY
> A MUSEUM
> A READING ROOM
> A BOOK-STALL FOR MAGAZINES AND NEWSPAPERS
> A CLUB
> A PLACE FOR PARTIES
> A REFRESHMENT BAR
> AN ORCHARD
> A ZOO
> AN AQUARIUM
> A VIVARIUM
> A HOME FOR PETS
> A PLAYING FIELD
> A GYMNASIUM
> • A BATHING PLACE
> A FAIR GARDEN
> A KITCHEN
> A DINING PLACE
> A LAUNDRY
> A FIRST-AID POST
> A CLEANSING DEPARTMENT
> STORE SHEDS FOR RAW MATERIALS

At the end of this stupendous list, the author, writing in 1952 noted, 'Prestolee, a one-time ordinary primary council school is now all of this'.

Review

These are the main themes of chapter M.

- In everything they do, children are searching for meaning; they are innately predisposed to make sense of their experience.
- Children sometimes surprise their educators by making meaning in ways that are seen as inappropriate, deviant, or just plain wrong.
- Attention to children's growing understanding, however inaccurate or incomplete it may seem, can give educators valuable insights into children's thinking and ways of making meaning.

 **is for Nel Noddings:**
learning to care

Who is Nel Noddings?

Nel Noddings is a professor of education at Stanford University, California and author of an inspiring book *The Challenge to Care in Schools*. Her formal biography lists her academic achievements, and her 15 years as a high school mathematics teacher, administrator and curriculum developer in public schools in the United States (equivalent to maintained schools in England). But Noddings writes primarily as a feminist, a philosopher, a mother, a compassionate and caring person, who is committed to the principle that the main aim of education is a moral one,

> *...to encourage the growth of competent, caring, loving and lovable persons.* 2002:94

An introduction to her work, by herself

> *In the 1992 introduction to this book* [The Challenge to Care in Schools: An Alternative Approach to Education] *I argued against an education system that puts too much emphasis on academic achievement defined in terms of test scores and the acquisition of information. Today* [2005] *the case could be made even more strongly. Students spend weeks – even months – preparing for and taking tests. Many of us believe that these are weeks that should be spent exploring new ideas, discovering new interests, extending established ones, and expressing thoughts in art, drama, music and writing. In particular we believe that students should be given opportunities to learn how to care for themselves, for other human beings, for the natural and human-made worlds, and for the world of ideas. This learning to care requires significant knowledge; it defines genuine education.*
>
> Noddings 2005a:xiii

What is the problem, as she sees it?

> *In general teachers may infer a need for children to learn the standard school subjects, while children – through their behaviour or verbalisations – express a need to learn how to live.*
>
> Noddings 2005b:148

> *"Why do we gotta study this stuff?" is a question that deserves an answer. ... What need is expressed here? Almost certainly, it is a need for meaning. Students need to know how schooling is related to real life, how today's learning objective fits into their own interests and plans, and even whether there is any meaning to life itself.*
>
> p.154

> *The original impetus to learn in early childhood – 'the need to engage in learning for its own sake' – gives way to 'a need that educators reward – the need to work hard for good grades.* p.156

> *If standard test scores rise, what real gain has been made?... Do we risk producing a generation of young adults whose attitude to learning and work will be just 'tell me what to do?* p.152

What is the alternative?

Noddings starts from the premise that 'there are centres of care and concern in which all people share, and in which the capacities of all children must be developed.' She distinguishes six centres of care, and argues that education should be organised around these six themes, rather than around the traditional disciplines. In brief, in her alternative model, all students would be engaged in a general education that guides them in:

- *caring for self*
- *caring for intimate others*
- *caring for strangers and distant others*
- *caring for animals, plants and the earth*
- *caring for the human-made world*
- *caring for ideas.*

A definition of caring

> The German philosopher Martin Heidegger (1889-1976) described care as the very being of human life. His use of the term is very broad, covering an attitude of solicitousness toward other living beings, a concern to do things meticulously, the deepest existential longings, fleeting moments of concern, and all the burdens and woes that belong to human life. From his perspective, we are immersed in care: it is the ultimate reality of life. ... This range of meanings will be of interest [as the discussion proceeds] but the meaning that will be primary here is relational.
>
> Noddings 2005a:15

In other words, Noddings emphasises, above all else, the relationship between the one who cares, and the one who is cared for; between the ones who care and the aspects of the world that they care for.

The six centres of care

Care for self: includes care for the physical self, for health and grace; care for the spiritual self, the questing searching, introspective self; care for the 'occupational self', the various interests, talents, skills and family duties of every student.

Care for strangers and distant others: includes caring at a distance, for global others; understanding the power of community and the dangers of erecting barriers against those outwith the community; keeping the lines of communication open between groups, opponents, nations; studying issues of race, ethnicity, religion, class and gender.

Care for the human-made world: the world of objects, tools, instruments. This theme includes learning how things work, a study that

> ...has to be related to how we want to live, to the obligations we feel as moral people, to our sense of beauty, to our desire to preserve the natural world.
>
> 2005a:142

It also includes maintaining, conserving, making and repairing, understanding and appreciating the things of the world.

Care for intimate others: how to live in caring relations, as friends, neighbours, sons, daughters, colleagues.

> If we regard our relations with intimate others as central in moral life, then we must provide all our children with practice in caring. Children can work together on a host of school projects...
>
> 2002:96

Care for animals, plants and the earth: includes a serious study of animals.

> Such study draws on literature, science, history, economics, politics, art, mathematics, psychology and religion, but it concentrates on a centre of care – on something that really matters.
>
> 2005a:131

It includes a study of plants, an opportunity to study response, beauty and interdependence: direct hands-on environmental projects; a reflective examination of one's own life, learning a sense of efficacy and responsibility.

Care for ideas: this includes Heidegger's deepest sense of care. Noddings elaborates,

> As human beings we care what happens to us. We wonder whether there is life after death, whether there is a deity who cares about us, whether we are loved by those we love, whether we belong anywhere; we wonder what we will become, who we will become, who we are, how much control we have over our own fate. For adolescents these are among the most pressing questions: Who am I? What kind of person will I be? Who will love me? How do others see me? Yet schools spend more time on the quadratic formula than on any of these existential questions.
>
> 2005a:15, 20

A book for children

Daddy's Lullaby

by Tony Bradman

A father arrives home late from work to find his baby awake and fretful. Together they check on the sleeping family, share a lullaby and finally fall asleep. This book is full of the loving language of parenthood.

Big ideas: family
gentleness
love
care

A book for educators

Changing the Educational Landscape: Philosophy, Women and Curriculum

by Jane Roland Martin

Jane Roland Martin is a feminist philosopher, rather than a mathematician, but her fine paper on Maria Montessori and the Casa dei Bambini in this collection of her essays has many connections with Nel Noddings' central theme.

Building on Dorothy Canfield Fisher's insight that the Casa dei Bambini should not be translated as 'The House of Children' because its real meaning is 'The Children's Home', Martin argues that the homelike qualities of Montessori's school are its distinguishing characteristics. For example, one key feature of Montessori's image of school as home is that the inhabitants of a school 'see themselves as a family...bound together by domestic affection'. At home, in the kind of home Montessori created in her school, children and adults alike feel secure, loved and at ease; they live in peaceful harmony.

Martin writes more extensively on these themes in her full length book *The School Home: Rethinking Schools for Changing Families*.

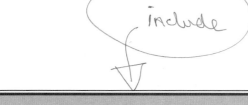

include

Review

The main themes of chapter N, written by Noddings herself, in a chapter called 'How to do it', are these.

How can we begin? Here's what I think we must do:
1. *Be clear and unapologetic about our goal. The main aim of education should be to produce competent, caring, loving and lovable people.*
[...]
5. *Give at least part of every day to themes of care.*
6. *Teach them that caring in every domain implies competence. When we care, we accept the responsibility to work continuously on our own competence so that the recipient of our care – person, animal, object or idea – is enhanced. There is nothing mushy about caring. It is the strong resilient backbone of human life.*

2005a:174-5

What do learners do?
Obedience versus desire **in learning**
Some thoughts on motivation

No amount of coaxing from his childminder could persuade nine month old Alex to release his hold of the TV remote control, stop pressing the buttons on it and exploring it with his mouth. A plastic toy replica did not satisfy him for long. His determination to find, reach and retrieve the authentic device was testimony to his desire to explore the real world.

Children into pupils

As every educator knows, it is not difficult to motivate young children; most of them are, most of the time, more than willing to comply with the wishes of their educators. Just as educators are kind and gentle with them, so they, in their turn, are kindly disposed towards educators, and respond to their directions, instructions, requests and routines, with every appearance of cheerful compliance. But maybe this willingness to please their kind and benevolent educators is not always entirely positive in its effects on children, who may, as a result, walk when they want to run, keep silent when they have important things to say, fall into line when they have their own ideas to explore.

A challenging study by Mary Willes, *Children into Pupils* (1983), illustrates this possibility. Having observed children in their first weeks in primary school, Willes concludes that the new condition of being a pupil requires children to submit to the rules of their classroom, both written and unwritten. She describes, for example, the unwritten rules that govern the times when the teacher talks to the whole class and invites responses.

> *The minimal inescapable requirement that a child must meet if he is to function as a participating pupil is not very extensive. It is necessary to accept adult direction, to know that you say nothing at all unless the teacher indicates that you may, to know that when your turn is indicated you must use whatever clues you can find, and make the best guess you can.* p.83

Her summary of the rule-bound nature of pupilhood is a gloomy one.

> *Finding out what the teacher wants, and doing it, constitute the primary duty of a pupil.* p.138

Willes' study shows a worrying side of the educator-child relationship; in her analysis the harmonious classroom is predicated on obedience. The educator directs; the child obeys.

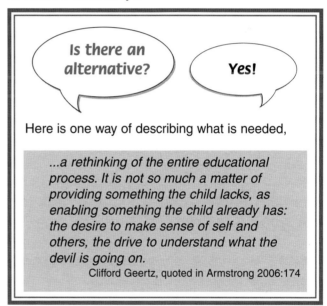

Is there an alternative? Yes!

Here is one way of describing what is needed,

> *...a rethinking of the entire educational process. It is not so much a matter of providing something the child lacks, as enabling something the child already has: the desire to make sense of self and others, the drive to understand what the devil is going on.*
> Clifford Geertz, quoted in Armstrong 2006:174

On desire

There are similar sentiments in the work of writer after writer. Some locate the capacity for desire in the very nature of childhood. For example, Susan Isaacs describes how

> *...the thirst for understanding springs from the child's deepest emotional needs... it is a veritable passion.* 1932:113

Others take a broader view; in a beautiful essay on the human condition the French philosopher Simone Weil writes,

> *In human effort the only source of energy is desire.* 1986:265

Knowledge versus desire

At a seminar on literacy, materials presented for discussion included a list of four kinds of knowledge that are drawn on in learning to read, namely:

- *linguistic knowledge*
- *psycho-linguistic knowledge*
- *socio-cultural knowledge*
- *situated and procedural knowledge.*

Maybe. This way of thinking about reading may be useful. But isn't it also possible to conceptualise the growth of literacy in terms of desire? The desire to crack the code, certainly, but so much more...

- *the desire to close the door on the everyday world and step into another*
- *the desire to create a story by reading it, to co-author it, along with the original writer*
- *the desire to meet new people, mythical monsters, witches, unicorns, the woodcutter and the prince*
- *the desire to repeat the experience over and over again, revisiting new worlds, new territories*
- *the desire to do all these things in the company of a loved one (parent, educator, keyperson, Grandpa), softly snuggled on someone's lap.*

A good question

Susan Isaacs (1930) tells the story of a child who appears in Piaget's work on children's understanding of causality, and of the way in which they learn the meaning, indeed meanings, of the word 'must'.

A child was told, "You must always put a 'd' in 'grand'".

[The French word 'grand' (big) not the English 'grand'.]

And he asked:

"Why, what would happen if you didn't?"

This child has already learned that some commands, and hence some forms of obedience, are not moral imperatives, but minor cultural conventions, which can, perhaps should, be questioned and challenged.

What Is and What Might Be

In this important book, the great thinker Edmond Holmes, writing in 1911, just after his retirement from the post of Chief Inspector of Schools, contrasts the lamentable condition of elementary education as he knew it, 'What Is', with one particular school, which he calls Utopia, but was a real school for all that (a village school in Sussex), and which he describes in the second half of his book, 'What Might Be'.

The Contents page reveals much about the themes Holmes will go on to develop:

In the closing lines of the book, Holmes spells out the significance of these terms, and presents his readers with a stark choice.

We must now make our choice between two alternatives. We must decide, once and for all, whether the function of education is to foster growth or to exact mechanical obedience. If we choose the latter alternative, we shall enter a path which leads in the direction of spiritual death.
1911:204

I want! I want!

In the Fitzwilliam Museum in Cambridge there is a beautiful engraving with this title, the work of William Blake, dated 1793. On a barren plain, a long, high, narrow ladder reaches far up into a dark sky studded with stars, till it touches a crescent moon. At the foot of the ladder, watched by two bystanders, a strange unearthly figure, maybe a child, sets one foot on the second rung of the ladder and looks intently upwards at the moon. It must be this figure that utters the cry "I want! I want!"

It is a beguiling and ambiguous image. Is it a representation of a child crying, in vain, for the moon, a child who is going nowhere, the incarnation of hopelessness? Or is it a child who desires to climb away, to soar above the earth, to reach the stars? Desire-for is very different from desire-to. The one expresses wanting in the sense of accumulation, having and grasping; the other embodies wanting as a form of energy, the energy that drives exploration, invention and imagination. Could schools and classrooms be re-formed so that children's desires (their desire-to) could be more fully respected and realised?

Six desires: more wise words from Edmond Holmes

Having described at length the profoundly anti-educational character of what was happening in the vast majority of elementary schools, Holmes outlines his alternative, which is based on a strikingly original analysis of the nature of children. He argues that children's learning and development is best conceptualised in terms of six 'instinctive desires', which 'no-one who studies the child with any degree of care can fail to observe'. These six instinctive desires are:

The communicative instinct – *the desire to talk and listen, which develops into the desire to read and write.*

The dramatic instinct – *the desire to play at make-believe, to imagine, to pretend, to identify one's life with others.*

These two may be grouped together as the **sympathetic desires**, in and through which the child grows in the direction of love.

The artistic instinct – *the desire to draw, paint and model, which grows into a restless desire to express and delight in a perception of visible beauty.*

The musical instinct – *the desire to dance and sing, to move and to express oneself with rhythm and grace.*

These two may be grouped together as the **aesthetic desires**, in and through which the child moves in the direction of beauty.

Duty and desire

Erich Fromm, in an otherwise gloomy indictment of the way we live now, *The Sane Society* 1956, offers a grain of encouragement. It is one of the functions of society, he argues, to shape the energies of its members in such a way that their behaviour is a matter of '*wanting to act as they have to act*' (his own emphasis). Goethe says very much the same thing.

> *Duty is when one loves that which one commands oneself to do.*   quoted in Nobel 1991:127

In the kindergarten

Mainstream educators visiting a Steiner Waldorf kindergarten are always struck by the absence of many aspects of classroom life as they know it. In particular, it is striking how rarely the kindergarten teacher issues commands. When it is time to tidy up, or to come indoors from the garden, the educator sings a particular song, or plays a tune, or herself initiates whatever it is that needs doing – setting chairs in a ring, or preparing the table for a meal. The educators talk, laugh and sing, but they never call for silence in which to make their wishes known. The silence that falls when a child lights the candle on the table before eating, or when the group is ready to start painting, or just before the fairy story begins, seems to arise from the children themselves, and not from the adult's injunctions.

The inquisitive instinct – *the desire to know the why of things, to understand how effects are produced, to discover new facts, and pass on, if possible, to their causes.*

The constructive instinct – *the desire to synthesise, to build things up, to put one's knowledge of the world to a practical use.*

These two may be grouped together as the **scientific desires**, in and through which the child grows in the direction of truth.

This is a fine example of how to 'rethink the entire educational process' as Clifford Geertz urges on page 64.

A *parent remembers...*

...the excitement and delight of my two children when they were invited to learn musical instruments. Rachel, aged seven, chose the piano and the cello, and Ben, aged nine, the drums and trumpet. At the start, both children had a similar experience, in spite of the differences between their instruments. They both returned from their first lesson with the same feeling of enthusiasm, thrilled by the possibility of mastery. As the weeks went by, they progressed from making musical sounds, a triumph in itself, to playing simple tunes. So far, so good.

However the time came when challenge outstripped enjoyment. Progress slowed down, the next steps became harder, practice did not make perfect. Inevitably, Rachel and Ben became frustrated. They came to a moment of choice: whether to continue, facing the risk of failure, and the apparently remote possibility of success – or to stop.

They never even considered giving up. Why? When learning became more difficult they began to understand what was happening: it wasn't that they were now 'no good at music'; they were still learning but now it was a challenge, although not an insurmountable problem. Adult encouragement, not pressure, was important.

The teacher's role was critical. Ben, for example, talked about music with Bernie, his teacher, who understood the kind of music Ben most enjoyed. He gave him music to play that matched his passionate interest in the rhythms of jazz.

Making music with others in the school orchestra, wind band and jazz band also motivated them. Playing together produced a volume and harmony of sound that could not be experienced as a solitary player. It offered an element of competition, as the children progressed through the ranks, becoming second, then first trumpet, sitting at the first cello desk. Rachel and Ben were part of a community of music makers. Their desire to learn was challenged by the difficulties they encountered: they needed encouragement to boost their desire. In the end, the challenges became a joy and desire triumphed over difficulty and despondency. Rachel and Ben went on learning, not because they had to, but because they knew they could.

A *learning story about obedient Neil*

Neil was six and a half years old when he completed this worksheet during a handwriting lesson.

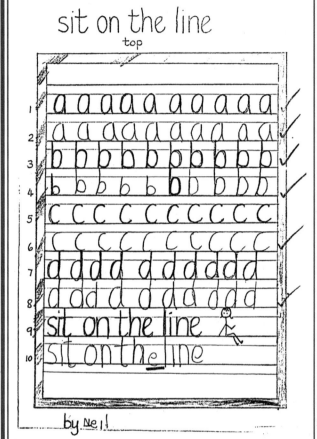

What a joy it is to see how he has enlivened this boring, dead-end, repetitive task with a tiny irreverent illustration; let's hope his teacher appreciated his witty commentary on this particularly undemanding demand on his time.

What is the moral of this story?
That when the spaces allowed for children's imagination, invention and creativity are small, children's powers to be their unpredictable selves are diminished, constricted and confined, but not extinguished. Neil's integrity as a thinker is untouched; he has found a minute gap in his teacher's plans for him, a pin-hole of an opportunity to express his own thinking, and his delightfully understated contempt for what he has been told to do. He has learned the lesson of obedience; but it has not quenched his desire to do more, to perform acts of literacy that will reveal his fine mind seriously at work.

A book for children

The Crane Wife
by Odds Bodkin

This Japanese folk tale tells how one stormy night Osamu the sail maker rescues an injured crane. Months later he offers shelter to a beautiful young woman caught in a storm. In return for his kindness she weaves him exquisite cloth, as light as a crane feather. From this, Osamu makes sails that fetch the highest prices and he grows greedy. His demands for more cloth lead to tragedy as the beautiful woman obediently gives all she has.

Big ideas: ambition
compassion
generosity
greed
the demand for
obedience and the
desire to please

A book for educators

The Play Way **by H. Caldwell Cook**

This extraordinary book is the bible of those who believe that children's play is not mere pastime, but one of the fundamentals of life. But its author was not a teacher of young children in preschool settings; in the years before and after the first world war, he taught boys aged seven to eleven at the Perse Preparatory School in Cambridge, boys in long shorts, woolly stockings and lace-up boots; he taught them every imaginable subject entirely through play, through, indeed, The Play Way.

The basis of his method was his recognition that interest must be the starting point. 'Let us remember that without interest there is no learning, and since the child's interest is all in play, it is necessary, whatever the matter in hand, that the method be a play-method.' And there is no difficulty in finding this interest, for 'it is the heart's desire we are born with'. It goes without saying that he makes no such claims for learning through obedience.

No summary can do justice to the contents of this book: more than 300 passionate pages proclaiming the author's creed; dozens of smudgy photographs of the boys playing with all their might; detailed descriptions of how it is all to be provided for and organised (for example, where to find the stiff coloured paper for making home-made books? From the grocer – the dark blue paper he uses for wrapping up sugar and tea.) And on virtually every page, an unforgettable reminder of the principle at stake.

> *When work and play are separated, the one becomes mere drudgery, the other mere pastime. Neither is then of any value. It is the core of my faith that the only work worth doing is really play; for by play I mean the doing anything with one's heart in it.*
> 1917:4

Review

These are the main themes of chapter O.

- There is more to being a learner than obeying the instructions of educators, however benevolent and well-intentioned.
- Worthwhile learning is not imposed on children from without; it is driven by inner desire – their passionate thirst for understanding.
- The desire to learn can be thought of as a form of energy, which drives exploration, invention and imagination.
- This energy can be constrained or constricted, but it is rarely, if ever, extinguished.
- Educators can choose whether to educate through obedience or desire.

is for principles of procedure:
the work of Lawrence Stenhouse

Introduction

Writing in 1975, Lawrence Stenhouse, Professor of Education and Director of the Centre for Applied Research in Education (CARE) at the University of East Anglia, opened his stinging critique of the objectives model of teaching and learning with a vivid glimpse of contemporary social history.

> *No issue has been more contentious in curriculum theory than the objectives model. At the 1972 Chicago Convention of the American Educational Research Association, participants displayed car bumper stickers reading HELP STAMP OUT BEHAVIOURAL OBJECTIVES! or HELP STAMP OUT SOME BEHAVIOURAL OBJECTIVES!*   p.70

As educators of all kinds know only too well, behavioural objectives, and their close friends and relations, attainment targets, desirable outcomes, learning objectives and early learning goals, did not get stamped out in 1972, or any other year. They are still alive and well, an inevitable part of any discussion of curriculum, pedagogy and assessment. But this is not for want of coherent alternatives, and Stenhouse will long continue to be remembered for his advocacy of just such a practical alternative. Not content with systematically demolishing the *objectives model* on a number of grounds, Stenhouse went on to unfold his arguments for a *process model*.

Stenhouse's best known work, *An Introduction to Curriculum Research and Development* (1975), in which he explains the process model, makes no specific reference to primary or early years education. It was written for teachers and other educators in the secondary sector, and his arguments are framed in terms of secondary students and the curriculum of the comprehensive school. Nevertheless, there are some striking parallels between Stenhouse's process model, its big ideas, and the approach we are presenting in this book.

The critique

Stenhouse identifies two fundamental objections to the universal application of the objectives model.

1) It mistakes the nature of knowledge by specifying in advance what learners should know, do and understand. Whereas it is the business of education to induct each generation of students, pupils and young children into the knowledge of our culture as a thinking system; it is the business of education to enhance the students' freedom and creativity as people, as learners and thinkers. He summarises this part of his argument in italics.

> *Education as induction into knowledge is successful to the extent that it makes the behavioural outcomes of the students*

In terms of early years and primary teachers' work today, Stenhouse's key point here is that it is impossible, in 'successful' education, to predict and control the learning outcomes, day by day, week by week.

His second fundamental objection to the objectives model concerns teaching and teachers.

2) It mistakes the nature of the process of improving practice. His argument here is that the objectives model attempts to improve the quality of education by increasing clarity about ends, defining ever more tightly the outcomes of the teacher's work, as seen in the behaviours of the students. This is not the way to improve the practice of teaching as Stenhouse sees it; he elaborates his view of teaching as a process that is both art and science, a process in which a good teacher is also necessarily a learner, in which inquiring, thinking pupils are taught by an inquiring, thinking teacher. Specifying in advance the end-points of such a process is no way to enhance its quality.

> *We do not teach people to jump higher by setting the bar higher, but by enabling them to criticise their present performance. It is process criteria which help the teacher to better his [or her] teaching... In curriculum development on a large scale the use of objectives laid down from the centre is a kind of teacher proofing... there can be no educational development without teacher development; and the best means of development is not by clarifying means but by criticising practice. There are criteria by which one can criticise and improve the process of education without reference to an end-means model.*   p.83

The process model

This model is Stenhouse's response to two big questions he sets himself.

> 🌿 *Can curriculum and pedagogy be organised satisfactorily by a logic other than that of the means-end model?*
>
> 🌿 *Can there be principles for the selection of content other than the principle that it should contribute to the achievement of an objective?* p.84

To both these questions, Stenhouse's short answer is, yes. He goes on to develop at some length the key features of the process model, which are, put very briefly, worthwhile content and principles of procedure.

Worthwhile content and what matters to children

Stenhouse explores the concept of worthwhile content by considering the criteria by which one could identify activities that are worthwhile in themselves. He is writing about the comprehensive school curriculum, remember, not primary schools or early childhood settings, but the list below will be surprisingly familiar to educators in these sectors.

The criteria include:

🌿 *that students are active rather than passive*

🌿 *that students are involved with real objects, materials and artefacts*

🌿 *that students are engaged in enquiry into ideas*

🌿 *that students follow purposes of their own, within relevant, meaningful activities*

🌿 *that students are involved in sharing, planning, and carrying out the activity with others.*

This list of worthwhile content has much in common with our understanding of *what matters to children*. Stenhouse's understanding of the learning that matters, that is worthwhile in itself, corresponds very closely to our emphasis on children exploring the world, thinking about the world and making sense of it.

*See also *the four domains of children's learning: what matters to children* on page 2.

Principles of procedure

Stenhouse develops this second strand of the process model in the context of the Humanities Curriculum Project (HCP) of which he was the director. This controversial secondary school project aimed to develop in students an understanding of social situations and human acts and of the controversial value issues they raise. The distinguishing characteristic of this project was the development of a discussion-based form of teaching and learning; the precise details of the approach are not relevant here, not least because it proved extremely difficult for many teachers to implement in practice.

What is relevant to primary and early years educators today is that Stenhouse set out to offer teachers some practical, pedagogical principles on which to draw in their work, general principles that would guide them in making the wise decisions and informed choices that lead to worthwhile learning. These principles of procedure were also to be used as criteria by which teachers could evaluate the effectiveness of their practice.

Principles of procedure and what matters to children

As briefly noted above, the early years professional community, and educators throughout the primary phase, are only too familiar with the ubiquitous objectives model. Over the years the labels have changed, but the underlying approach is the same. First define the learning that is to be done by each and every child; then devise a programme that will make sure it happens. The work of Stenhouse reminds educators that there is a viable, coherent alternative, though it is by no means an easy option.

We have written this summary account of Stenhouse's process model because we believe that both strands of the model have much to offer primary and early years educators today, especially in terms of the challenges that some educators seem to experience in prioritising process (the ways in which children learn) over content and product (the outcomes of children's learning). It is worth remembering that *Starting with Quality* (DES 1990), the sadly neglected Rumbold Report, advocated just such a distinction and just such a priority.

> *The process of education – how children are encouraged to learn – is as important as, and inseparable from, the content – what they learn. We believe that this principle must underpin all curriculum planning for the under-fives.* p.9:68

We have already noted some parallels between worthwhile content and *what matters to children*. Here we suggest some principles of procedure that educators today might consider discussing in their staff groups, before reformulating a set of principles of their own, on which to base their developing practice, and for use as process criteria in the review and evaluation of quality in their schools and settings.

The principles presented here are not new. They are indeed 'old certainties taken in new directions', as Vivian Gussin Paley pointed out in her encouraging letter (2005) to the authors of *First hand experience: what matters to children*. They represent our best effort to support educators in thinking through the quality of their practice

Children learn most effectively when:

- ❧ they are actively engaged with first hand experiences, materials, persons, places, living things, that introduce them to the world outside the setting

- ❧ they play, explore and investigate, using all their senses, collaboratively and independently, with no fixed objective, goal or standard to limit their learning

- ❧ they are given generous allowances of time and space for their learning

- ❧ they use their fertile imaginations as a way of exploring the possibilities of the world and what might happen in it

- ❧ they feel secure, valued and confident within the harmonious society of the setting

- ❧ they encounter big ideas that are relevant and meaningful to them

- ❧ they have multiple opportunities to put their experiences into words, freely using spoken language for a wide variety of purposes

- ❧ they have opportunities to use 'the hundred languages of children', the expressive languages in which they represent their ideas – in dance, paint, clay, pencil, song – and every kind of material

- ❧ they are taken seriously and properly supported by their educators as passionate and committed learners.

Of course children learn in other ways, at other times, in other conditions. They learn when they are passive, goal-driven, when they meet dead-end ideas, and go unrecognised as original thinkers. They learn when they are labelled high or low ability. They learn when they are told they are lazy, careless, average or slow. They learn when they are sitting silently, constrained from expressing their own ideas and inventions.

But these are the wrong kinds of learning. The principles of procedure we have listed above are a summary of our best understanding of how educators can work in the interests of children and their worthwhile learning.

We hope the list will stimulate educators to define for themselves the principles that will support them in making the wise choices that are always theirs to make, whatever framework they work with.

A book for children

The Fossil Girl

by Catherine Brighton

This biography of Mary Anning, born in 1800, is told in comic strip format. She had a passion for fossil hunting among the cliffs of Lyme Regis, for which she ultimately became famous, astonishing the pre-Darwin scientific world with her great discoveries. At the age of 12 she found the first ichthyosaur in England, and later a plesiosaur, which took her 10 years to dig out.

In Stenhouse's terms, Mary's learning was active, purposeful and real. She had time and space for her explorations and her discoveries were taken very seriously indeed by geologists.

> **Big ideas:** persistence
> purpose
> discovery

A book for educators

Research as the Basis for Teaching: readings from the work of Lawrence Stenhouse

by Jean Rudduck and David Hopkins

Stenhouse's best known work, *An Introduction to Curriculum Research and Development*, has been selectively quoted, and reduced to a minimum in this chapter. For those who wish to pursue his thinking at greater length, this collection of readings is highly recommended. Jean Rudduck and David Hopkins have selected papers that represent the big ideas in Stenhouse's life's work; they have chosen passages that are, in their own words,

> *...characteristically energetic in their stalking of powerful ideas and characteristically striking in their articulation of those ideas.*
>
> p.4

Review

These are the main themes of chapter P.

- The work of Lawrence Stenhouse offers a practical alternative to the objectives model of teaching and learning: both strands of the process model are relevant to early years and primary educators today.
- The concept of worthwhile content has much in common with our understanding of *what matters to children*.
- The concept of principles of procedure can be used by educators to define their own principles, to guide them in the choices and decisions they make in the interests of worthwhile learning.

What do learners do?
Learners question and answer

Questions and answers: enquiry in daily life

Children never stop asking questions, although they do not always ask them out loud, and some questions may not be the ones that adults expect. Questions are an important part of adult lives too, ranging from small everyday trivia to world affairs. Problems big and small are resolved through asking questions and discoveries are made through seeking answers.

Questions and answers in the work of three scientists

"My work is very exciting when I'm on location. Sometimes we don't know what we'll find, so the main questions are:
    What have we got here?
    What are its main properties?
    How does this material suit what the customer needs?
Even though we can have a set plan and direction' they usually get in the way. We need to be free to explore what is around us and take it from there. Back in the lab things can be routine but you have to be free enough to expect the unexpected and follow new leads. Something you're very familiar with can sometimes surprise you."

Adam, chemical engineer

"Some people might look at what I do and think it's not much. It's slow and time consuming. Tiny details, or just one question, can absorb you for days and you need freedom of time and sometimes from others too, to really get involved in a project. Don't get me wrong, I do need others in my work - we bounce ideas off each other and disagree a lot. But I also need my own thinking time. Having time to think and reflect is very important to me."

Mary, soil analyst

"I get involved with the causes of road accidents. Was an accident caused by the condition of the surface? Maybe we have a theory, but can we prove it? Sometimes we go down a blind alley and it seems like maybe we've wasted time, but actually that blind alley is always worth exploring. What we find out there might not be relevant to the investigation in hand, but it might be useful another time; we never know what the next problem will be."

Kiran, forensic scientist

A culture of enquiry

Scientists observe, ask questions, predict, hypothesise, investigate, communicate and evaluate - all key activities in a culture of enquiry. Other key features of their work include:

- having a genuine purpose
- looking for evidence
- being able to deviate from a plan
- taking time
- going down blind alleys and storing knowledge for another time

- having space and resources to work on the project
- having time to think alone
- looking and listening, attending to details
- bouncing ideas off others

Can these features be used by educators as the basis of a culture of enquiry for children?

Children's questions

Children's natural disposition to ask big questions will be nourished in a culture of enquiry in which educators value children's questions and support them in finding answers.

> **Are there monsters in the dark?**

Children aged four to six discussed what frightens them, stimulated by a child remembering a recurring dream about monsters. Over time a lot of children admitted to being afraid of the dark, and discussed their theories about what scared them.

Educators responded to these discussions by bringing in torches and yards of material for children to make dark places: under tables, dens, tents and caves, indoors and outdoors. On late afternoons there were torch-lit story sessions; children listened to books and poems about darkness and the sounds of night; they went on torch-lit walks in the school building and school grounds.

Weeks later a happy mother visited her child's class teacher to say, "What have you done to my daughter? She slept with the light off last night for the first time. I'm so amazed and pleased."

Children's questions about the dark were taken seriously by their educators: children were supported in finding answers. Months later, there are still dark places and resources in their classroom for children to test out theories about darkness; they ask for stories about the dark; going on night-time walks in the winter has become a regular event in their curriculum.

Gregory's big questions

Children aged between nine and eleven met in a museum studio for an introduction to a study day. They discussed things that you can see and things you cannot; they were introduced to the idea of images symbolising invisible concepts such as love, right (as opposed to wrong) and God: Christian cross, Islamic moon and star, Jewish star.

Then the visit began; in the Islamic gallery, Gregory, aged ten, put up his hand and said, "The thing is… I mean, what's it all about? Why are we here?"

A couple of days after the visit, back at school, Gregory recorded his thoughts on the class tape recorder.
 "Hello this is Gregory… I've come up with some questions.
 Do animals have religion?
 Could there be a bee with… a Jewish bee or something?
 And… why are we here? Was it an accident? Was it an invasion?
 Do we really know how it all began?
 Could it have been a mistake?"

Gregory has embarked on what Robin Alexander, later on page 77, calls a 'chain of enquiry and understanding' which may well occupy him for many years to come. He has invented his own big questions, which none of his educators can answer for him.

Catching children's questions: building a culture of enquiry

Two of the authors worked with a group of educators on an in-service course over several months. One educator, Gemma, working with four and five year olds, started collecting children's questions; support staff joined in and very soon they produced a book of children's questions.

Reflecting on these questions, Gemma noted that many of them were questions to which children already knew the answer. For example, Anann asked, "Do snakes eat crabs?" and promptly answered himself, "Yes they do. I saw a snake eat a crab on T.V, but only some do."

Other questions and answers recorded in the book had been discussed in small groups.

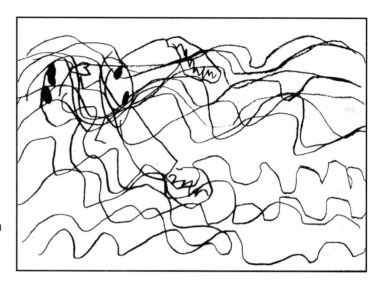

Do snakes eat crabs?

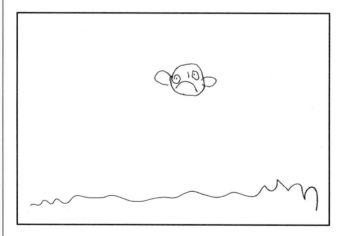

Are bees afraid of water?

Kai asked, "Do bees fall from the sky into water and die?" After discussion children reached a consensus and agreed, "Bees just fly about and are actually afraid of water".

Michelle's question, "Why is the sky blue?" was considered by a small group of children. Suzanne's answer, "Because there are no other colours" was accepted by them all and was the only answer to be recorded in the book.

Encouraging children to ask questions and openly valuing them are certainly important in developing a culture of enquiry, but Gemma was not convinced that simply recording children's questions and answers was enough. She returned to the book of questions and identified some that children could investigate for themselves.

She decided to act as a model, using children's questions as a starting point and asking for their help in seeking answers. Her plan was to confide in the children, saying something like this, "I've been looking through our book of questions and I'm very interested in Suzanne's idea that the sky is blue because there are no other colours. I've been wondering… is this right? Can you help me find out?"

Although Gemma planned to organise 'sky-watch' teams who could mix colours to match the sky and record their results, she was fully prepared for children to come up with their own ideas for worthwhile enquiries.

Some children might be more interested in looking for frightened bees and checking whether they ever fall from the sky or fly above water. Could they prove that bees really are afraid of water?

Questions and answers: the traditional view

In the traditional view of talk between an educator and a child, it is the educator who asks the questions and the child who answers them. But what are these questions really for?

The short transcript that follows comes from a significant small-scale study comparing four year old children's talk at home and at nursery school. It was carried out in the early 1980s, but is by no means out of date in its insights into the different kinds of talking and thinking in young children's lives.

Child: Can you cut that in half? Cut it in half?
Teacher: What would you like me to do it with?
Child: Scissors.
Teacher: With the scissors? [Child nods] Well, you go and get them will you?
Child: Where are they?
Teacher: Have a look round. [Child goes over to the cupboard, gets some scissors] Where do you want me to cut it?
Child: There.
Teacher: Show me again, 'cos I don't quite know where the cut's go to go. [Child shows teacher where she wants paper cut] Down there? [Child nods; teacher cuts child's piece of paper in half] How many have you got now?
Child: [No reply]
Teacher: How many have you got?
Child: [No reply]
Teacher: How many pieces of paper have you got?
Child: Two.
Teacher: Two. What have I done if I've cut it down the middle?
Child: Two pieces.
Teacher: I've cut it in…? [Wants child to say 'half']
Child: [No reply]
Teacher: What have I done?
Child: [No reply]
Teacher: Do you know? [Child shakes head]
Other child: Two.
Teacher: Yes, I've cut it in two. But… I wonder, can you think?
Child: In the middle.
Teacher: I've cut it in the middle, I've cut it in *half*! There you are, now you've got two.

Tizard and Hughes 1984:194-5

In this brief exchange the educator's purpose is clear: her string of questions is intended to elicit the one word answer 'half' from the child, presumably in the interests of extending her mathematical vocabulary. In her pursuit of this goal, however, the educator has overlooked the child's original request, which plainly shows she knows very well what a half is. Here the educator's questions serve no genuine purpose; indeed, their only effect is to confuse the child who has opened the exchange by spontaneously using the very concept that the teacher appears to be trying to teach her.

But there is an alternative to this pointless pattern of exchange between adult and child: a different relationship, a different kind of encounter, where both adults and children ask interesting questions and discuss each other's answers. This is not an impossible dream. As long ago as 1980, a small scale study by David Wood and his colleagues showed that educators who asked the most questions were themselves asked the fewest questions by their children. In contrast, children asked many more questions and offered their own ideas more freely when interacting with educators who asked few questions.

The alternative: 'chains of enquiry and understanding'

What would happen if both questions and answers were to be more equally distributed between adults and children? Robin Alexander describes just such a state of affairs in his powerful pamphlet, *Towards Dialogic Teaching* (2006) which bears the challenging sub-title 'Rethinking classroom talk'.

Alexander calls for talk to be reinstated as the core of the curriculum.

> *Reading, writing and number may be the acknowledged curriculum 'basics' but talk is arguably the true foundation of learninng.*   p.9

But it is not the educator's talk which is to be of paramount importance: it is the children's talk, both questions and answers, which are to become the 'true centre of gravity' of every learning exchange. Alexander explains that

> *...important though* [the teachers'] *questions are we could profitably pay no less attention to children's answers to our questions and to what we do - or more commonly, alas, fail to do - with those answers.*   p.25

He describes how such a change in practice could come about,

> *If we want children to talk to learn – as well as learn to talk – then what they say probably matters more than what teachers say. So it is the qualities of extension and cumulation which transform the classroom talk from the familiar closed question/answer/feedback routine into purposeful and productive dialogue where question, answers and feedback progressively build into coherent and expanding chains of enquiry and understanding.*   p.26

Choices for educators responding to children's questions

When faced with difficult questions, such as those asked by Gregory, on page 74, educators have choices. They can:

- *take the easy option, dismiss the question and hope it goes away*

- *accept it is a valid but difficult question that many people have dedicated their lives to answering*

- *acknowledge that there are many different viewpoints and invite other children's contributions*

- *invite further exploration, encouraging what Alexander calls 'purposeful and productive dialogue'.*

Some of these options clearly do much more than others to develop and sustain an culture of enquiry. Educators will be guided in their choices by the value they place on children's questions, their interests and concerns.

Celebrating children's questions

Educators can go some way to establishing a culture of enquiry by celebrating children's questions as positive contributions to the thinking of the whole group.

Annabelle Dixon worked as a teacher for many years and always kept a Question Book, recording children's questions. She valued these questions highly and used them as a rich resource in her teaching.

> *I wanted to push the edges of [the children's] learning on as far as I could. In order to do this I needed to know what it was they wanted to learn. The questions they were asking became one of my tools for finding this out. Above all it helped me find out their level of thinking... I couldn't work without them as a guide, aid to reflection and source of feedback.*
>
> Rich et al 2005:72

Children loved referring to the class Question Book. Sometimes they chose which questions they wanted to investigate and sometimes they brought their parents in to show them what was in the book. Their enthusiasm set off a chain reaction and their enquiries spilt over into their home lives.

Children's questions as starting points for learning

Children's questions are invaluable starting points for learning. Indeed, Ruth Griffiths, author of an incomparable study of children's imagination, goes further. She argues that it is children's questions that show educators the way to an entire curriculum.

> *Out of the questions of children shall we gradually come to discover what are the essentials of a perfect curriculum.*
> 1930: 331

Asking questions in play

Children go on asking questions beyond the gaze of their educators, who can choose whether to respond to these or not.

Three weeks after a school visit to the museum at Verulamium, St. Albans, nine year old Martin and Georgiou were still playing at Romans whenever they met up outside school.

They were wondering, 'What does Roman food taste like?' There was only one way to find out. They made up their own recipe based on what they had learned from books and their museum visit. They finally persuaded Georgiou's mother to buy each of them a herring to try out their recipe.

> **The ingredients**
> **One herring**
> **Almonds**
> **Honey**
> **Grapes**
> **One dormouse *(if you can find one)**
>
> **What to do**
> **Cover the herring in honey**
> **Stick almonds on the outside**
> **Stuff the herring with a dormouse, or just grapes**
> **Bake it in a hot oven**

At Georgiou's house they prepared the food, cooked it and, dressed in togas, ate it, taking photos to show the class. Although the teacher's planning had ended with the museum visit and the class had moved on to a new topic, it became clear that several other children, as well as Georgiou and Martin, continued to be interested in Roman life in Britain. In response the teacher returned to the topic.

Some children wanted to set up a Roman kitchen role-play area, which they did. Some wrote their own Roman recipes to try out at home and school, some opted to try the herring dish for themselves, all culminating in the production of *A Roman Cookery Book for the Present Day*. Some children began to reflect on other aspects of the museum visit: they made wax tablets to write on, just as Roman children did; they made Roman style sandals, sturdy enough to wear: they wrote poetry inspired by the idea of Boudicca's attack on Verulamium. One boy, previously a reluctant writer, wrote a poem with the unforgettable beginning, 'In the Roman city flames rise the colour of blood…'.

Their teacher reflected, "It was as if a light had gone on when I heard Georgiou talking about the herring. I'd just rushed them on to the next topic and there was so much they still wanted to find out. The museum visit had inspired them so much and I'd have been mad to just lose all that enthusiasm. Looking back I remember that it had been hard to shift Martin and Georgiou from the Roman kitchen in the museum. They were fascinated by the recipes there, and I kick myself for not picking it up sooner. When they brought in the photos everyone erupted with their own interests - jewellery, shoes, writing… they'd taken in so much. I never realised. It really taught me a lot. I'm grateful to Georgiou and Martin."

* They couldn't find a dormouse.

Comment

In settings without opportunities to explore questions that matter to children, there are unlikely to be motivated, engaged learners, willing to take risks, persist and go in unexpected directions. But these are the learners who will one day become scientists, designers, doctors, engineers, economists, film directors, architects, composers, philosophers – maybe even teachers.

Developing a culture of enquiry: what can educators do?

The educators' task is to provide opportunities for children to do the things that scientists do, including:

- 🍃 enquire with a genuine purpose in mind
- 🍃 hypothesise and look for evidence
- 🍃 deviate from a plan
- 🍃 go down blind alleys and store knowledge for another time
- 🍃 take time
- 🍃 use relevant resources, including people, for their enquiries
- 🍃 attend to details
- 🍃 think alone
- 🍃 bounce ideas off others.

The questions below offer some useful discussion points for educators developing a culture of enquiry:

- 🍃 Do educators respond honestly to children's questions?
- 🍃 Do educators treat children's questions as more important than adults' questions?
- 🍃 Do educators value children's non-verbal questions as well as their spoken questions?
- 🍃 Do educators support children whenever they raise difficult issues?
- 🍃 Do educators use children's questions as starting points for learning?

A book for children
Why do the stars come out at night?

by Annalena McAfee

A child questions his grandfather and receives poetic, imaginative answers, rather than facts. This book encourages children to invent their own creative answers to such questions as:

> 'Why is the sun hot?
> Why is the sky so high?
> Why is grass green?'

There are many ways to answer a question and many possible solutions to a problem. This book values divergent thinkers.

> **Big ideas: playing with ideas**
> **the limits of reason**
> **inventiveness**

A book for educators
Towards Dialogic Teaching

by Robin Alexander

This booklet, from which several quotations in this chapter are taken, is an enormously helpful summary of the vast research literature on the place of talk in learning, the kinds of talk that matter most, and what educators can do to foster the most worthwhile talk. Readable, succinct, scholarly and humane, Alexander's 'work in progress' as he calls it, is fuelled by a passionate and political concern for the current state of primary and early years education, caused, he argues, by a centralising and controlling government. The only antidote, he maintains, is a democracy, whose citizens can

> *…argue, reason, challenge, question, present cases and evaluate them… democracies decline when citizens listen rather than talk, and when they comply rather than debate. True democracy subverts authoritarian tendencies.* p.53

Review

These are the main themes of chapter Q.

- 🍃 In their explorations children seek answers to their big questions; they ask about what matters to them.
- 🍃 Children's questions, verbal and non-verbal, and their answers, need to be taken seriously, highly valued and used as starting points for further enquiry.
- 🍃 In a generous environment children love to ask big questions: a culture of enquiry is essential for the growth of children's powers as thinkers.
- 🍃 A culture of enquiry can extend beyond settings, in children's homes and communities.

What do learners do?
Learners *represent* **their learning**

The significance of children's representations

Luckily for their educators, children's learning, laid up in their heads and hearts, does not remain there, invisible and out of reach. Learners long to bring their learning out into the open for their friends, parents and educators, to share, to compare, to connect, to enjoy and admire. What is more, they do so in a brilliant variety of ways.

Educators everywhere are gradually becoming more familiar with one of the key concepts at the heart of the curriculum and pedagogy of educators in Reggio Emilia, Italy, now commonly known as the Reggio approach. Reggio educators frequently speak of the 'hundred languages of children', a phrase which they use to refer to the many symbolic languages in which children represent their growing fascination with and understanding of the world. But it is not just in the pre-schools and infant/toddler centres of Reggio Emilia that children represent their learning in these hundred languages. In every setting, school and classroom where the conditions are right, children express their learning in ways of their own invention, using paint, clay, ink, talk, photography, dramatic play, writing, music, computers, dance – and more. It is through the respectful and attentive study of these representations that educators can come closest to seeing, appreciating and understanding the richness and variety of children's learning.

The hundred languages of Reggio Emilia: the fantastic theory

Some comments from Carlina Rinaldi.

> There is something else that is full of democracy, the theory of the hundred languages of children. It should be developed more and more because it is fantastic. Nobody has understood the power of this theory... I see the hundred languages as a lake with many, many sources flowing into it. I think that the number of a hundred was chosen to be provocative, to claim for all these languages not only the same dignity, but the right to expression and to communicate with each other.
> 2006:175, 193

Representations in play

Some pages in Jean Piaget's great work on play, *Play, Dreams and Imitation in Childhood* (1951) are dense with polysyllabic abstractions. There is, for example, an alarming diagram of the schemas of assimilation and accommodation, mapped across three stages of development: it is hard to relate all this to the lives of children. But other pages come alive with copious, lovingly observed descriptions of the play of his daughters and son. Here, for example, is Jacqueline, not quite four years old.

> At 3.11, she was impressed by the sight of a dead duck which had been plucked and put on the kitchen table. The next day I found J lying motionless on the sofa in my study, her arms pressed against her body and her legs bent. "What are you doing, J? – Have you a pain? – Are you ill?"
> "No, I'm the dead duck."
> p.133

And here is Lucienne, a little older,

> At 4.3, L standing at my side, quite still, imitated the sound of bells. I asked her to stop, but she went on. I then put my hand over her mouth. She pushed me away, angrily, but still keeping very straight and said "Don't. I'm a church."
> (the belfry)
> p.125

These extracts are not just entertaining glimpses of the Piaget household; there is more here than the amusing sight of the great Professor's attempt to silence his child's unwelcome noises. Here we see two children re-enacting recent events in their lives, events which have had significance and meaning for them, and are then played out, re-presented to whoever is there to see them. These re-presentations are themselves significant; they signify the children's interest in the original event, and their desire to understand it. (Or, in Piaget's terms, they are evidence of the processes of assimilation and accommodation.)

It is important to remember that the clumsy English title of the book from which these observations are taken, *Play, Dreams and Imitation in Childhood*, bears no relation to its original French title: *La Formation du Symbole*. From this rather different perspective, the snapshots of Jacqueline and Lucienne at play are seen as part of Piaget's 'big idea'. His argument is that in play, children learn to think symbolically, using their bodies or their toys, a banana, a pillow, a blade of grass, almost anything that comes to hand, to represent, symbolically, in another form, the events, ideas and experiences that matter to them. Indeed, it is in this volume that Piaget defines symbolic play as 'a form of thought'. Lucienne's and Jacqueline's symbolic play alerts us to their powers as thinkers; their play is the language in which they represent and express their thinking.

Representing learning in blocks

On a trip to Paris, Davey, nearly three years old, was fascinated by the Eiffel Tower which he saw illuminated with golden lights against a clear black sky. There was an impressive full moon shining behind it. Davey talked about this scene on the journey home; the brightness and shape of the moon, the blackness of the sky, the size and colour of the Eiffel Tower.

At home he built his own tall tower with wooden blocks, making several attempts to build it, as he said, "Bigger than me, bigger than Mummy and even bigger than Daddy… and," he insisted, "...there has to be a full moon shining."

He chose a grapefruit to represent his full moon because, "It's big and a bit like silver."

Davey named his construction "My silver and gold" and was keen to recreate it at his nursery.

R is for remember

In a moving short story by the writer Grace Paley, a grandmother, Ruth, is celebrating her 50th birthday and waiting for the arrival of her daughter Sara.

At six, Sara and Tomas with Letty, the first grandchild, standing between them, would be at the door. Letty would probably think it was her own birthday. Someone would say, What curly hair! They would all love her new shoes and her newest sentence, which was Remember dat? Because for such a long time there had been only the present full of milk and looking. Then one day, trying to dream into an afternoon nap, she sat up and said, Gramma, I boke your cup. Remember dat? In this simple way the lifelong past is invented, which, as we know, thickens the present and gives all kinds of advice to the future.
[Two hours later...] But it was six o'clock and the door bell rang...The door had barely opened when Letty jumped forward to hug Ruth's knees. I'm gonna sleep in your house, Gramma.
I know, darling, I know.
Gramma, I slept in your bed with you. Remember dat?
Oh sure, darling, I remember. We woke up around five, and it was still dark, and I looked at you and you looked at me and you had a great big Letty smile and we both just burst out laughing and you laughed and I laughed. I remember dat, Gramma. Letty looked at her parents with shyness and pride. She was still happy to have found the word 'remember', which could name so many pictures in her head.

1985:25

This enchanting story within a story, which we have appropriated here as a learning story, a story about representing learning, reveals the significance of the act of remembering.
And indeed, the significance of learning to name that act with the words 'Remember dat?', mastering the act that can 'name so many pictures', people, places, joys and sorrows, in children's lives. Remembering is part and parcel of children's representations.

Ducklings and big ideas

Three and four year old children in a nursery had patiently watched over an incubator full of duck eggs. When the ducklings emerged, there was intense excitement and attentive observation. The children watched. They touched. They talked about what they saw and felt. They took photos and printed them. They looked at books about ducks. And talked and touched and watched some more. Then they started to represent their learning, to express their growing understanding of the duckness of duck. They did drawings of ducks and paintings of ducks and they sculpted ducks in clay.

What's going on, when children of three and four model a duckling in clay?
What big ideas might they be struggling to represent? Some possibilities:

- *the relation of the parts to the whole*
- *the living detail of an organism*
- *function and form*
- *beauty*
- *pattern*
- *the translation of the inner (image) to the outer (model).*

Max and Daniel talk about drawing and writing

Max and Daniel are seven year olds who do a lot of drawing. Max explains to his teacher, Mary, how he feels about drawing.

> *You can put a lot of life into drawings if you try. Then it feels as though it's really happening. If you get into drawing, it feels as though it's really happening.*

Max's drawing is the domain where his imagination makes things really happen. School and home are real too, of course, but if you get into drawing 'it's really happening.' Both Max and Daniel use writing and drawing as parts of the same process, building imaginative worlds of their own. They talk to their teacher about this process.

> *Max: I draw my pictures before I start writing.*
> *Daniel: Me too.*
> *Max: So then I can write about my picture.*
> *Mary: Does it help you to write stories?*
> *Max & Daniel Yes.*
> *Mary: Do you think you could write a story without drawings?*
> *Daniel: I think I could – probably.*
> *Max: I don't think I could do it properly without a drawing by the side.*

Later in the same long tape-recorded discussion there is even more telling evidence of the importance of drawing to their intellectual and emotional well-being, to their lives and learning.

> *Mary: What would you say if you were told you could never, you were never allowed to do any more drawings?*
> *Daniel & Max: (as if in pain) Oh!*
> *Daniel: Leave school.*
> *Max: I don't know.*
> *Daniel: I would go, er...*
> *Max: I don't know but I just wouldn't do anything else. I would get very upset and start shouting at whoever said that.*

Drummond 2003:134

Representing understanding in talk

A class of four and five year olds had been studying the human body, including the digestive system. The two educators who worked together in this class wanted to document the learning that had gone on during this period of study; they used a video camera, a tape recorder, camera, collected drawings, models and made detailed observations.

They were very disappointed with Heather's drawing which seemed to show a limited understanding. But when one of the educators sat down with Heather to talk about her picture, they were forced to revise their judgement.

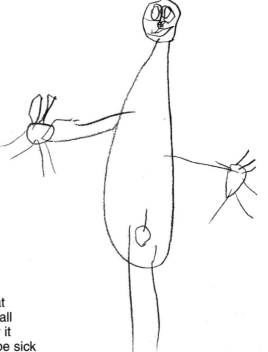

E: Can you tell me about the apple in your picture, Heather?

   (silence)

E: Where did the apple start its journey in your body?

H: Well, when you first take the apple and bite it – you need to use your teeth to bite it because they are sharp and apples are good for your teeth and if you don't keep them clean they will all fall out and maybe they'll never ever grow back again.

E: So when you have bitten the apple, what happens next?

H: Well, next you have to chew it and swallow it of course. You have to chew it up really really into small pieces or else it doesn't fit down.

E: Down where?

H: Down your throat and into your tummy. There are tubes that go all the way down here in your tummy. They are very small so that's why you have to chew. If you didn't chew properly it might not go down your tubes and then you could maybe be sick even.

E: So what happens next?

H: The bits of the apple that we don't need come out in a poo.

E: And the rest of the apple?

H: All the good bits float away into your body and help you to run faster and grow up to be strong. My brother, he is very strong, he doesn't like apples though. He loves bananas!

Representing learning in sand

Some children from a small rural school lived on farms or had farm workers in their household. During an outbreak of foot and mouth disease, children aged five to seven, played in a sand area at their nursery. They gathered farm animals and put them in the sand. They sorted out a group of horses, sheep, cows and hens. The hens were placed in the sand, and set on their way with the instruction, "Off you go to peck".

The remaining animal groups were each carefully covered in sticks and small twigs. The children lit an imaginary match and took it to the base of each pile. They dug holes and pushed the animals in, covering them with sand and a final flourishing tap of the spade with an announcement, "NOW WASH YOUR HANDS".

Seven magnificent words

A class of nine and ten year olds in a middle school had been studying the concept of historical time. At the end of the unit of study, the class teacher asked everyone to spend 10-15 minutes writing down what they had learned. She spoke quietly to one member of her class, a child identified with special educational needs, who, her assessments showed, was barely reading or writing independently. She assured him that he need not complete the task in writing, but could dictate his thoughts for her to scribe. To her surprise, he refused, and said he would write about his learning like everybody else. To her even greater surprise, he produced the magnificent seven word sentence shown below.

> Time is sumting you cenot Get a Ginn

What is the moral of this story?

- *That even beginning writers may know more than they write?*
- *That even inexpert and inaccurate writers may have big, important ideas to communicate?*
- *That educators should be very slow to assume that secretarial skills develop in strict parallel with thinking skills?*
- *That judgements about children who find writing (or reading or adding and subtracting) very difficult should not blind educators to their powers as thinkers, or to their capacity to represent their thinking in ways of their own invention?*

Yes, all of the above – and more.

Time is sumting you cenot Get a Ginn

Representing learning through drawing

> *Children use drawings as a tool for understanding and representing important aspects of their own personal lived experiences of people, places and things... Their representations [also] serve the function of exploring 'big ideas' common to all our lives, like dependence and dominance, good and evil, danger and adventure.*
>
> Anning and Ring 2004:26

Drawing what happened

David, nearly four years old, was involved in Peter Pan role-play. It included flying lessons, Peter leading Wendy, John and Michael on their journey from London to Neverland accompanied by Tinkerbell, then finally a boisterous scene where the Lost Boys meet with Peter and together they fight a tattooed man.

When the play subsided David wanted to draw what he was playing.

The drawings are a vivid representation of his deep involvement in the adventure story.

The role of the educator

- 🌿 To provide *all kinds of materials in abundance, a rich palette of resources, available and accessible at all times.*

- 🌿 To organise *time and space. Slow time and large spaces, for second thoughts, for revisiting, for revision and repetition, for discussion and debate, for solitary thinkers and doers, and for small groups of collaborating children.*

- 🌿 To value *the spontaneity, variety, unpredictability and richness of children's representations. How? by discussing them, 're-presenting' them ("tell me some more about what you did yesterday"), visibly, audibly, demonstrating the value educators put on them.*

- 🌿 DO: *trust that there are meaning and purpose in what children do in their representations – of whatever form, shape, size, in whatever medium, whatever symbolic language.*

- 🌿 DON'T say:
  "That's lovely dear, what is it?"
  "That's lovely dear, put it on the shelf."
  "But horses aren't purple."
  "No, that's not what I wanted."

- 🌿 REMEMBER: *children's representations offer educators unparalleled insights into children's thinking and understanding. However unexpected, contrary or apparently chaotic, they are always worth taking seriously.*

A book for children
The Legend of the Indian Paintbrush
by Tomie dePaola

This legend tells of a small boy with a gift for making beautiful representations of his world, rather than for the more traditional pursuits of his tribe. Through the wise intervention of his elders he comes to value himself and what he has to offer.

> **Big ideas:** contribution
> difference
> integrity
> self worth

A book for educators
Drawing and painting in Early Childhood: Children and Visual Representation
by John Matthews

In this book, John Matthews emphasises the importance of children's representations as they develop their understanding of the world

> *…when they represent anything (using a mark, a shape, an action or an object) they make something stand for something else, and through expression (in speech, action or images) they show emotion.*   p.1

Matthews documents in detail the journeys taken by his own children, from birth to 19 years, showing how, where and why children make drawings and paintings, and how educators can support them. This is absolutely not a book that tells educators how to teach children to draw a cat. Through this book, educators come to value the many and varied ways in which children represent their own experiences of cats…and 'cars on a road', 'a man digging in the ground for bones of animals', 'the journey from nursery to home', and 'a footprint on the moon'.

Review
These are the main themes of chapter R.
- 🌿 Children represent their learning in a remarkable variety of ways.
- 🌿 In children's representations, attentive educators can see their growing understanding of big ideas and the growth of their powers: to remember, to reflect, to explain, to invent, to make unexpected connections.
- 🌿 The educator's responsibility is to provide generously for children's representations, to organise time and space for their thinking and doing, and to value what children do.

What do learners do?
Learners make stories

Making stories: part of everyone's life

Making stories is not just for well known authors, like Jeannette Winterson; everyone makes stories. Making stories helps to justify actions, cope with events, make better decisions, explore reality, get nearer to the truth and feel more at peace with their world.

> The journey would have been a nightmare every morning if I'd got that job.

> I'd better wear this dress because I think they're arranging a secret party for me. There's bound to be all my old friends, good music and masses of champagne.

Most people fondly remember making stories in their childhood. Today's children do exactly the same; exploring big questions, 'Who am I?' 'What do I do here?' 'How would it be if I were someone else?' 'What if?', addressing what matters to them.

Gathering material for making stories

Everything children experience can be stored away and used for making stories. They collect what Michael Morpurgo (2007) calls 'seedcorn' from which stories can grow; not just out of extraordinary events, but from regular everyday experiences: the mundane, the joyous, tragic and traumatic. Children never stop collecting seedcorn for stories, even from turbulent experiences; they may be making meaning of violent home lives, war-torn communities or racial intolerance.

Libraries of books, as well as experience, are essential in a generous environment, if children are to become confident in making their own stories.

> *To have read widely and deeply, to have soaked oneself in the words and ideas of other writers, to have seen what is possible and wonderful, to have listened to the music of their words and to have read the work of the masters must be a help for any writer discovering his own technique, her own voice.*
> Morpurgo 2007:25

The role of educators is to offer a generous and nourishing environment of rich experiences which can become the source of new stories.

The impact of listening to stories

Children learn a lot about making stories whenever they listen to them.

> *Long before I wrote stories, I listened for stories. Listening for them is something more acute than listening to them. I suppose it's an early form of participation in what goes on. Listening children know that stories are there. When their elders sit and begin, children are just waiting and hoping for one to come out, like a mouse from its hole.*
> Welty 1985:14

Even with experience of the world, access to books and story tellers, it may take time for children's own stories to ripen. Other children make stories immediately, in direct responding directly to the materials and situation at hand.

Where do children make stories?

Children make stories everywhere, out and about, at home and in settings, as they play with whatever they find: natural materials, role-play resources, small worlds, blocks, paint, mud and boxes.

Children choose to represent their stories in many ways: painting, drawing, writing; sometimes children make their stories with their whole bodies, especially in a spacious outdoor environment.

Making stories: using objects on the beach

Two year old Douglas makes a story of his new experience, making sense of it as he plays with stones, sand and the sea. Sitting on the beach he picks up three pebbles and names them, "Daddy, Mummy and Douglas. All at the beach". He digs a small hole in the sand and fills it with water. As he places each stone into the tiny pool, trying to do so before the water drains away, he says, "Daddy in, Mummy in and Douglas in". Next he moves them all around saying, "Swim, swim, wheee!" He jumps the *Douglas' stone* out, saying, "Ahhh, no like it," and laughs loudly, jumping the stone in and out of the water, repeating his words.

Big ideas in Douglas' story	What matters to children
family	*having a sense of big belonging*
identity	*being in different kinds of places*
togetherness	*moving about in the world, touching the world*

Developing as a story maker

In his nursery, three year old Vasos used one prop, a police helmet, in his solitary play. He often walked up and down, patrolling silently, playing his simple story, 'There was a policeman.'

Vasos made a more complex story when he was joined by Christopher, who usually played a robber or a monster; now there are two characters in the story, 'There was a policeman and a robber'.

The boys became 'play buddies' and often played together. The stories they made became more complex; they developed a relationship between their two characters, invented a scene for play and a simple plot which they played over and over again, 'Christopher the robber robbed a house. Vasos the policeman came and locked him up. He went to prison for a very long time.' Play allowed them to explore what mattered to them.

Big ideas in Vasos' and Christopher's story	What matters to children
good and bad	*finding out how to keep safe in the world*
justice and injustice	*who is in the world*
consequences of actions	*making sense of the world*
imprisonment	*being with friends*
power	
fantasy and reality	
enveloping and enclosure	

Respect for children as story makers

Few people treat the stories of children with greater respect than Vivian Gussin Paley, whose work is described in chapter B. Encouraging children to tell stories, giving them time and space, listening with dedication and an interested ear, she writes their stories down, reads them back, and invites children to recreate them in play. Like Paley, educators can choose to write down the stories of children to both make them permanent and give children high status as authors. In her acceptance of all play themes, she values every child's contribution. She insists that no child should ever be excluded from playing and telling stories and would welcome the themes in Vasos' and Christopher's' play.

> *Story telling is easy to promote when there is a tangible connection to play.* 1984:2

'What would happen if I found a wolf?'

After listening to the music *Peter and the Wolf* by Prokovief, Jamie aged three, leapt up and said, "I think I saw a wolf!" He set off on a wolf hunt around the nursery garden, calling to his followers, "Use your wings to magically fly, fly, fly if you are in danger," urging them on. When Jamie reached the end of the garden he called to a man digging in an adjoining allotment. "Have you seen a wolf?" "None here today," called the man. Jamie shouted back, "Man. What's your name?" Imagine his surprise when the man replied, "Peter." At this the children were off flying again in case the wolf was near.

Being able to fly is an ingenious way to escape from a wolf. Inspired by this story in music, Jamie picked up the seedcorn of 'a wolf' and drew on his recent introduction to the world of wolves and hunters, as well as his abundant experience of stories, to make the exciting wolf hunt story that he played with his friends.

Big ideas in Jamie's story

danger and safety
strangers
escape
fantasy and reality

What matters to children

finding out how to keep safe in the world
being with friends
being in the world of living things

What an opportunity for an educators to catch Jamie's story, tell it back to him and his co-players, then go on to turn it into a book for him, 'Jamie and the Wolf Hunt', played by Jamie, Simon, Vijay, Dylan, with special guest, Peter.

Making stories = storying

> As children, every time we told an experience or tried to express our feelings about something, we were storying, and through storying we built our sense of who we were. Rico 1983:52

> I want to suggest that stories have a role in education that goes far beyond their contribution to the acquisition of literacy. Constructing stories in the mind – or storying as it has been called – is one of the most fundamental means of making meaning; as such it is an activity that pervades all aspects of learning. Wells 1987:194

Storying is important to children. If children can play a story, they are more likely to be able to tell a story. Playing stories, and then telling stories (or the other way round), will lead some children on into a passionate desire to represent their stories in writing.

But without an abundance of ongoing play experiences throughout their childhood, some children may never be motivated as willing story makers when it comes to writing stories their down. Even when children do go on to write, it is very important that they keep on playing and making stories in their play.

Magic and Mysteries by Taylor

In the introduction to this story, Taylor, aged 11 rejoices in the power of words to weave magic. She writes,

You may not know deep into your mind there is magic and definitely mysteries. Maybe gooley or catchy, maybe pretty or spooky, but definitely mysteries to be solved. Something swirls round and round in circles, this is the magic to solve your mysteries. This story is definitely gooley, catchy as well, spooky in some places but not pretty. Don't worry, I'll be with you through all of this story...

<u>**Or not!**</u>

Big ideas in Taylor's introduction
The power of words

What matters to children
finding out how to keep safe in the world

Noor's story

Noor arrived at school one morning demanding paper and pencil. It was urgent. She folded the paper and made a book. On the cover she drew a soft, white furry rabbit, and dictated the title, 'My rabbit'. She drew a second picture of her rabbit on the inside and asked the teacher to write, 'My little rabbit has died'. Then Noor toured the school stopping every adult who had time to listen (and several who did not) and read her story.

With a pencil, a few words and a helpful educator, Noor could describe the brief life and sudden death of her rabbit. She could explore the finality of death; she could share this with many people and know that the written story would ensure her rabbit was not forgotten.

Big ideas in Noor's story	What matters to children
death	being in the world of living (and dead) things
grief	understanding how the world works
loss	
caring	

The influence of other story genres on children's stories

Children's stories reflect not only their own experiences but also other story genres: fairy tale, fable, myth, adventure, mystery, comic book, fantasy and poetry. Familiarity with the many genres of story increases children's capacity to make a growing variety of stories.

Dan's story

Dan, aged seven, has been influenced by the genre of creation myths. He tells a story using paint to depict mysterious mountains, red, orange, brown and gold. His teacher asked if there was a story to go with the painting and Dan dictated the following,

> "At its beginning the divine serpent carried God here and there in its mouth.
> The mountains opened where they stopped at night to rest."

In his short creation myth Dan explores what matters to him as he muses on mysterious, possibly incomprehensible ideas.

Big ideas in Dan's painting	What matters to children
creation	making sense of the world
awe and wonder	make my own world map

When children make stories they explore the same rich themes that occur in stories by adults, which deal with big ideas such as:

> belonging, responsibility, courage, fear of the unknown, love, hate, compassion, loneliness, friends, enemies, reconciliation, justice and retribution, being lost and loss itself.

No wonder children love to listen to stories and make their own; they are an essential way of making sense of the world, reflecting their desire to understand and bring order out of chaos.

Katherine's story: One Moonlit Night

Katherine, aged ten, wrote about the weak triumphing over the strong in her carefully crafted story which she illustrated herself.
It was published in *A Box Full of Stories.* (1995).

Natty shivered. She curled her long tail around her. Natty was a mouse.
The moon shone into her burrow in the middle of the cornfield. Far away the church clock struck midnight. Time for a midnight feast! Natty scrambled up to the burrow entrance and slipped out into the night.

Although it was summer the night was cool and there was a light breeze.
Climbing up a corn stalk Natty could see all the way to the village.
As she munched away at the corn, Natty felt sure she heard something. But as she couldn't see anything, she turned back to her meal.
Then EEEEeeekkk!!!

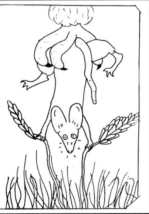

Natty felt herself being lifted up. She opened one eye. Two huge talons surrounded her. She bit one of them hard.
With another deafening screech the owl dropped her.
She was a bit bruised, but otherwise unhurt.
Natty looked up to see the great bird sail across the moon as the dawn came.
Slowly Natty crawled back to her burrow, curled up in the straw and fell asleep.

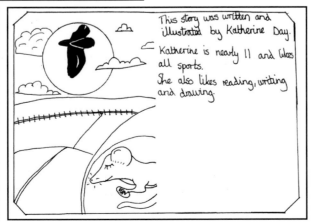

This story was written and illustrated by Katherine Day.
Katherine is nearly 11 and likes all sports.
She also likes reading, writing and drawing.

Learning from children making stories

When educators take the stories that children make seriously, they can learn more about

- 🌱 **what children know and the limits of their knowledge**
- 🌱 **the powers of their spoken and unspoken languages**
- 🌱 **what they want to find out more about**
- 🌱 **what interests them**
- 🌱 **what they have experienced and how they feel about it**
- 🌱 **what they are concerned, anxious or worried about**
- 🌱 **how they see themselves in the world**
- 🌱 **what they know about stories and story making**
- 🌱 **what matters to children.**

Big ideas in Katherine's story
danger
ecosytems
ecology
food chains
fortune or instinct
survival

What Matters to Children
being in the world of living things

finding out how to keep safe in the world

A book for children

Imagine a Day

by Ron Gonsalves

This is a book of paintings with the added lustre of a brief poetic phrase. Each picture is a springboard for making stories, inviting the reader to climb into reflections of trees, to build viaducts with acrobats and generally do the impossible.

Big ideas: **adventure**
making new worlds
trying out ideas
daring

A book for educators

Singing for Mrs Pettigrew: a story-makers' journey

by Michael Morpurgo

Michael Morpurgo has an unparalleled reputation as a writer for children and for recognising *what matters to children*. He was the Children's Laureate in the U.K. from 2003-2005. In this book he describes himself as a 'story-maker' and traces his development from being uninterested in books, to discovering writing as his voice, becoming a prolific writer of stories for children. He explores how writing stories enables him to make meaning of the world.

Each story in this collection is concerned with difficult issues, such as death, war, unkindness, hatred; they have been written to bring children face to face with aspects of a hugely disturbing world, where they can explore big ideas and what matters to them.

Each story is prefaced by a description of how and why Morpurgo came to write it, outlining memories of past experiences and influences from the world which inspired them. It is not only Morpurgo's real experiences that have influenced his stories, but the documented experience of others too. His own library of books has been essential to him.

Morpurgo's conviction that making stories and telling stories is for everyone, is an inspiration for both educators and children.

Review

These are the main themes of chapter S.

- Children make stories everywhere, with a variety of materials.
- When educators take children seriously their story making flourishes.
- Making stories enables children to make sense of the world, explore what matters to them and understand big ideas.
- Children need both first hand experiences and opportunities to listen to stories, so that they have rich resources on which to draw for making stories.
- Time and space for play support children's growing power to make stories.
- Children's stories offer educators valuable insights into their learning.

Jason and Mahatma Gandhi

Eight year old Jason was studying India at school. As he sat alongside his teacher, looking through various resources for the topic, he came across a photograph of Mahatma Gandhi; he became very interested in him, wanting to know who the man was and why his clothes were so different from his own. Jason started to research Gandhi's life and, being severely dyslexic, there came a moment of choice: how was he to represent his learning?

His teacher provided three dimensional media and taught him some modelling skills; he chose to work with a huge lump of clay. Jason became totally absorbed with it; he spent three whole days making a sculpture of Mahatma Gandhi. He missed assemblies; he had to be encouraged to take a break for lunch and was first through the classroom door every morning. Jason was so engaged he hardly spoke to anyone. He occasionally asked for technical advice from his teacher and acknowledged the admiring comments of other children.

At last the sculpture was finished and Jason carefully placed the final embellishment, a pair of spectacles made from fuse wire. Jason stood proudly by his model. He had become an artist, respected by the rest of the school community.

A week or so later his class visited London's Commonwealth Institute: there in the entrance hall to the museum was a larger than life-size statue of Gandhi, cast in bronze. On seeing this, Jason's scream of delight silenced all the visitors. He stood in front of it in awe and said, "Someone has copied my sculpture!"

Without time to research the life of Gandhi, to investigate the properties of clay, to work with total absorption, without interruption, to realise and refine his sculpture in all its final glory, Jason would never have had the deep satisfaction and delight of achievement. He had not only learned about a great human being, but was able to take time representing this learning through his sculpture.

Big ideas encountered by Jason
leadership and humility, representation, achievement, pride, self belief

A time to weep and a time to laugh

Some experiences have a great impact on children's lives: loss, sickness, death, war. Children need time to assimilate these into their understanding of how the world works. Sometimes it will be many months before such experiences can be resolved through their play and representations.

In *The Colour of Home* by Mary Hoffmann, Hassan, a child escaped from war-torn Somalia, paints his home as he last remembers it: engulfed in flames, destroyed and ugly.

Only slowly, with the compassionate understanding of adults and other children in his school, can Hassan come to experience joy in his new home.

A day at the Casa dei Bambini, 1913

The current obsession with haste is not new. Dorothy Canfield Fisher visited Maria Montessori's school in Rome, in 1913; she describes her impatience with a group of four and five year old girls as they set the table for lunch.

I was watching the four little girls who had now at last finished their very leisurely meal and were preparing the tables for the other children. They were about four and a half and five years old, an age at which I should have thought children as capable of solving a problem in calculus as of undertaking, without supervision, to set tables for twenty other babies. They went at their undertaking with no haste, indeed with a slowness which my racial impatience found absolutely excruciating. They paused constantly for prolonged consultations, and to verify and correct themselves as they laid the knife, fork, spoon, plate, and napkin at each place. Interested as I was, and beginning, as I did, to understand a little of the ideas of the school, I was still so under the domination of my lifetime of over-emphasis on the importance of the immediate result of an action, that I (felt the impulse) to snatch the things from their incompetent little hands and whisk them into place on the tables.

But then I noticed that the clock showed only a little after eleven, and that evidently the routine of the school was planned expressly so that there should be no need for haste.

The phrase struck my mental ear curiously, and arrested my attention. I reflected on that condition with the astonished awe of a modern, meeting it almost for the first time. "No need for haste"- it was like being transported into the timeless ease of eternity.

And then I fell to asking myself why there was always so much need for haste in my own life and in that of my children? Was it, after all, necessary? What were we hurrying to accomplish? I remembered my scorn of the parties of Cook's tourists, clattering into the Sistine Chapel for a momentary glance at the achievement of a lifetime of genius, painted on the ceiling, and then galloping out again for a hop-skip-and-jump race down through the Stanze of Raphael. It occurred to me, disquietingly, that possibly, instead of really training my children, I might be dragging them headlong on a Cook's tour through life.

pp.22-24

The time of life

Nearly 90 years later, Carlini Rinaldi is passionate in her argument that learning takes time.

Today there is too little talk about schools and time. For me it is important that for a school to be a place of life, then it needs the time of life, and that time of life is different, for example, to time of production. In production, the most important element is the product... In a school what is important is the process, the path we develop.   2006:207

If schools are to become places of real life experiences, where what is on offer really matters to children, rather than brief encounters with a series of units always with an eye on coverage and the clock, then these experiences will need generous time, the time of life, as Rinaldi calls it. Then learning will be deeply understood and become part of the whole child, rather than a thin veneer.

The sound of silence

Children need stimulation and guidance, but they also need time to themselves. Is it appropriate for them to escape from the material world to the world of silence and day dream? Or are children simply wasting time when they do this?

Time spent alone, or in daydreams, may provide a necessary lull in the rhythm of the day.

A space and place where children can choose to be silent and alone can be organised with soft cushions, a small sofa, a deep chair, a rug over a table, a bedspread and a clothes airer, dens in the garden, enclosures made from branches and twigs.

Such places are invaluable for imagining. Here stories are woven, plans laid, inventions dreamed up. Children can think and solve problems.

Time to build a trolley: a nursery educator tells a tale

When the children came out into the nursery garden, first thing in the morning, they saw two enormous cardboard boxes, just delivered, and asked what was in them. "We've ordered something from the catalogue. We've left it for you to unpack and put together."

Children set to work opening the boxes; the packing tape was strong and resistant. Joshua fetched a pair of scissors from the trolley we kept outside and began to cut through the tape. Jade and Katie, trying to open the second box, looked over to see what Joshua was doing; they knew he was good at solving problems. Off they went to get a pair of scissors for themselves and opened their box too.

Looking at the assorted pieces children began to talk about what it might be. Matthew thought it was a football net, perhaps because he was passionate about football. But Amina was quick to recognise the parts and confidently announced that it was "a new outside trolley".

Matthew had an idea for fixing it together and ran to get a roll of masking tape from the old trolley. As he returned triumphantly waving the tape, Trishelle stared at him in disbelief. She was just about to tell him "No!" but stopped and composed herself. She had learned that people need to have a go, that trying is important. Trishelle patiently held onto her end of one part of the metal frame as Matthew

wrapped tape around three more pieces. "Right!" he announced as he finished, "Let go!" The children let go and Matthew's construction crashed to the ground. Trishelle paused for a moment then said, "There might be nails in the box…" There were no nails, and no instructions, but there was a small spanner and a packet of nuts and bolts.

Before the children began to put the frame together, they had to work out which bit went where. This was difficult for them, and we wondered how long to leave them without help. We were just about to step in when we heard Amina telling the others they could look at the old trolley to "see how it goes". She wheeled the old trolley over and set to arranging the pieces, lining up the holes, threading the bolts through and screwing on the nuts.

There was only one spanner, so they took turns with it. Some children held the frame in place while others began to bolt it together. They made sure all the nuts were tight, crawling under and over to check the hard to reach ones.

At long last the trolley was finished. The children had taken their time: we could have helped them and hurried them – but what for? They were learning to persist and persevere, to take responsibility for their shared project. And they succeeded.

Less is more

Spreading time thinly across a multitude of topics gives learners little opportunity to follow new paths, to discuss, reflect, evaluate, to try things out, to take a risk.

But with generous allocations of time, less becomes more. The more time that is spent on fewer worthwhile projects, the greater the depth of understanding for the learner. Learning is returned to the learner.

What can educators do for joined-up learning?

Staff in one school have taken the decision to heal a fragmented timetable by creating big blocks of uninterrupted study time. They have given themselves the freedom to work on one subject area for a week at a time – or even longer. Now it is common practice for a class and their teacher to spend two whole weeks on an art project, a science investigation, or an in-depth study of an interesting local landmark – and naturally these sustained enquiries reach far

beyond any traditional subject boundaries. Furthermore, this generous allowance of time provides opportunities for children both to build on their previous knowledge and to explore the chosen subject through talking, drawing, writing, debating, through music, drama and dance, through background reading, hypothesis and experiment. A recent inspection evaluated the learning in the school as 'outstanding'. Of greater importance is the children's love of learning.

Time with owls

Children aged five spent time with owls, watching and listening. They made sketches, detailed paintings and wax resist pictures from real-life observations. Some made fabric pictures, and others soft sculpture nests to use in their play. They listened to stories about owls and studied them.

Teachers observed that children, in particular those whose first language was not English, were more motivated than ever before to talk and write whenever the subject was owl related.

What matters to children

being with living things

finding out what is in the world

How is it possible to provide and organise for time?

🌿 *Spend more time on fewer projects. Select from the multitude laid out in the various curriculum documents, and take time to explore them in many dimensions, building in first hand experiences from the real world and responding to them in a variety of ways and with a range of media: in pictures, graphs, charts, models, written and spoken words, music, dance and drama.*

🌿 *Plan for continuous rather than fragmented learning by blocking time. This gives children the flexibility to pursue a project rather than having it cut short at the ring of a bell or the hand of a clock. Perceive time as a whole rather than as a series of episodes.*

🌿 *Make time available for children to think, plan, discuss, decide, try out their ideas, evaluate and change them.*

🌿 *Respect and value children's day dreaming time, often the genesis of deep thinking, a new idea or a moment of enlightenment.*

🌿 *Model the time needed to complete a task; such as reading a story, or at least a whole chapter of a novel to a class of eleven year olds, or becoming engaged in siphoning water out of a water tray into buckets with a group of four year olds.*

🌿 *Plan projects that take time:*
       plant a garden and harvest a crop of vegetables: cook and eat them
       design and make a book with hard covers and sewn pages, a real book for a real purpose, such
       as a poetry anthology, a novel, a record of current research
       make a hypothesis and set up tests to prove or disprove it
       solve a real problem that urgently needs a solution
       learn to play a musical instrument.
In each of these projects children will encounter big ideas, but without time to reflect on their learning they will not know they have met them.

🌿 *Organise for a flexible approach to planning and time-tabling that will give educators opportunities to collaborate.*

🌿 *Value the time spent on observing and recording children's learning, all the way along the learning journey, and not just at the end.*

A book for children

The Time of the Lion by Caroline Pitcher

Joseph's father had warned his son not to seek the company of the lion, for the time was not right, but Joseph ignored his father's advice and secretly spent many hours with the lion and his family, learning to respect their ways. When the traders came to the village, bartering with Joseph's father for lion cubs in return for their beads, Joseph believed his father had betrayed the lion.

Little did he realise that his father had been working secretly with the lion to protect the cubs. Little did Joseph's father realise that his son was old enough and trustworthy enough to share his deep respect for lions.

How long does it take for a father to know his son?
How long does it take for a son to know his father?

Big ideas: conservation
care for the planet
relationships
trust
the time being ripe

A book for educators

Shoe and Meter by Marina Castagnetti and Vea Vecchi

This book has an impressive sub-title: *Children and measurement, First approaches to the discovery, function and use of measurement.* But it is far from being a dry-as-dust treatise on early mathematical education. It is a lively, engrossing example of what the Reggio educators call 'documentation', the process of making learning visible.

A class of five and six year old children in a Reggio preschool need another work table, identical to the others in shape and size. They call in a carpenter, who agrees to make it for them, if, and only if, they give him the precise measurements. Six children volunteer for the job of measuring the table: they work on this project every day for about an hour. It takes ten days before they are satisfied that their measurements are accurate enough.

This extended time-scale is an important part of the project. Along the way the children have many startling ideas and unexpected adventures; they use every different kind of measuring tool, including Tommaso's size 29 shoe, which confusingly measures 20cm, and which nearly trumps the meter stick that the educators, controversially, refrain from advising the children to use as the correct, standard instrument. Loris Malaguzzi, founding father of the Reggio approach, comments,

> ...the greater the challenge, the more tenacious the children become, and moments of serious concentration alternate with moments of playful exploration together, all with the utmost enjoyment.
>
> p.17

Reading about this project is every bit as serious, concentrated, playful and enjoyable.

Review

These are the main themes of chapter T.

- When children take time with their learning they encounter the big ideas of trust, responsibility, self belief, perseverance.
- Taking time to be in the world matters to children.
- Taking time is essential for children to develop their ideas; to dream; to heal.
- Educators can provide and organise generous allocations of time.

What do learners do?
Learners thirst for understanding

Relearn the Alphabet by Denise Levertov

> U
> relearn the world, the world
> understood only in doing, under-
> stood only as
> looked - up - into out of earth,
> the heart an eye looking,
> the heart a root
> planted in earth.
>
> 2003:76

In our first book, *First hand experience: what matters to children,* we used the poem, 'O taste and see' by Denise Levertov to introduce an alphabet of learning from the real world.

In another poem by Levertov, 'Relearn the alphabet', each stanza focusses on a letter of the alphabet. In the stanza *U for Understand*, the poet again speaks of the centrality of doing in learning, 'the world understood only in doing'.

The world understood only in doing

This principle was behind a new wave of thinking about primary education during the late 1960s and early 1970s, when active learning was promoted to develop mathematical and scientific understanding.

In America

Frank Watson, former Executive Director of the Vermont Institute for Science, Math and Technology reflected on the excitement of working at the Elementary Science Study in the 1960s.

> *Rather than beginning with a discussion of basic concepts of science, ESS (Elementary Science Study) puts physical materials into children's hands from the start and helps each child investigate through these materials the nature of the world around them. Children acquire a great deal of useful information, not by rote but through their own active participation… it is apparent that children are scientists by disposition. They ask questions and use their senses as well as their reasoning powers to explore their physical environment; they derive great satisfaction from finding out what makes things tick; they like solving problems; they are challenged by new materials or by new ways of using familiar materials.* 1996

How does light bend?

In England

While Watson was working in America, in the UK in 1966, excited by the new Nuffield Science and Mathematics programmes, a class of nine and ten year olds were investigating rays of light. Shoe boxes were collected to create dark chambers through which beams of light from torches could pass. One boy borrowed a smoker from his grandfather, a bee-keeper. Each shoe box chamber was filled with smoke and beams of light projected through a small hole in the side of the box. With amazement the children could see the path of light as it travelled from the torch through the smoke filled box, unaware that the smoke had leaked out of the classroom, down the corridor and into the headteacher's study. The fire service was alerted and fire fighters arrived to track down the source of the fire. They found children alight with the joy of discovery. The children KNEW that light truly travelled in straight lines. They had seen it with their own eyes. Their wonder increased as they repeated the process with a glass convex lens placed inside in the box. This time the ray of light bent as it met the lens. Why did it do this? How did it happen? They could see that it did happen, but why? This was the start of a quest that led the children to investigate places where lenses are found, the eyeball (involving dissection), spectacles, magnifiers, binoculars and to make connections between them.

In the introduction to his *Theory of Colours* Goethe (1810), wrote

> *For merely looking at an object cannot be of any use to us. All looking goes over into an observing, all observing into a reflecting, all reflecting into a connecting and so one can say that with any attentive look we cast into the world, we are already theorising.*
>
> 1970:xi

Activity and exploration: a new approach to mathematics

In 1970, reflecting the pioneering work of The Nuffield Foundation, E.M. Williams and Hilary Shuard based their approach to teaching mathematics on the growing understanding that children learn through real experience.

All mathematics starts for children with encounters with the world, and with the exploration of its behaviour. Abstraction and generalisation are late stages in a process which starts with handling, doing and talking. This process cannot be completed, and a child cannot grow to full mathematical maturity, unless both aspects, the real and the abstract, have been explored and knitted into one whole. p.442

A spirit of enlightenment was sweeping through the education community. A series of books for children, *Nuffield Primary Maths, 5-11*, was published in 1979 by the Nuffield Foundation. Children learned by handling and investigating. Expecting children to learn without understanding was no longer acceptable practice.

In contrast:

In *Hard Times* by Charles Dickens (1854), Mr Thomas Gradgrind, the schoolmaster, believes children to be

...little vessels... ready to have imperial gallons of facts poured into them until they were full to the brim... Teach these boys nothing but facts. Facts alone are wanted in life. Plant nothing else and root out everything else.

He accosts Sissy Jupe, the daughter of a horse breaker and circus trainer.

"Girl number 20...give me your definition of horse". (Sissy Jupe thrown into the greatest alarm by this demand.) "Girl number twenty unable to define a horse!" said Mr Gradgrind... "Girl number twenty possessed of no facts in reference to one of the commonest of animals."
"Some boy's definition of a horse. Bitzer yours..."
"Quadruped. Graminivorous. Forty teeth, namely twenty-four grinders, four eye-teeth and twelve incisive. Sheds coat in the spring; in marshy countries sheds hoofs too. Hoofs hard but requiring to be shod with iron. Age known by marks in mouth."
"Now girl number twenty," said Mr. Gradgrind. "You know what a horse is." pp.11-12

40 years on:

Nathan Isaacs (1895-1966) reflects on his early experiences with number:

As a small boy I took quite kindly to counting and elementary number ideas; but at some time in my first few school years I started falling behind. I remember vividly puzzling my head about the reasons for what we were being taught, and being unable to see them; but it did not seem to occur to the teacher to stop and explain, so my mind just stayed blank and bewildered, and I failed to do my sums. It worried me to be unable to keep up with the other boys, and all the more because I liked figures; but there I was. Then one day came the blinding flash of the obvious. It suddenly occurred to me that perhaps one could learn the rules for doing sums without stopping to understand them first. Perhaps that was what the other boys, or anyway some of them, did. I tried this out and it worked like magic. I was soon holding my own with most of the others, and after that, in the matter of arithmetical performance, I never looked back. But I recall that for some time a haunting sense of having cheated remained. Hardeman 1974

The search for understanding

Children are determined to make sense of the multitude of experiences they meet each day. Every experience has to be fitted into their frame of reference. If they have not met anything like it before they will try to find a similar experience to which they can connect it, which will help them understand it.

Children's observations and explorations of the world all contribute to their growing understanding of the world, its universal features - and its differences. They make generalisations that form a part of their world map.

Luke learning to understand human anatomy

Luke, nearly three, was in the park with his grandmother and the family dog, Badger. Luke watched Badger intently for some time and then suddenly turned to his grandmother and said, "Grandma we've got arms". "Yes we have," replied his grandmother, "We have two arms." Luke continued, "I've got arms. You've got arms. Badger hasn't got arms; that's why he carries the stick in his mouth."

A few months later

Luke, now three years old, was leaving the nursery after a happy morning. He explained to his mother that he had had a wonderful time and couldn't wait to return. His mother explained that he would not be coming back the next day; as they left, his mother said, "Say bye-bye to nursery. Wave bye-bye nursery, we'll see you on Monday." "No mummy," replied Luke. "I can't say bye-bye to nursery." "Why not?" asked Luke's mother. "Because you can only say bye-bye if you have eyes, a nose and a mouth." Luke demonstrated quite clearly his understanding of the futility of addressing inanimate objects.

Through his experiences Luke was developing a growing understanding of the big ideas of similarity, difference, possible and impossible, alive and inanimate. He checked each new experience against previous ones, asking himself, as it were: how does it fit? Is there a pattern here? How can I explain it?

Rebecca learning to understand the language of school

Rebecca, aged four, had just started school. Her teacher had shown the children the main features of the classroom they would be sharing together, and explained that because there was no school hall they would have P.E. on the grass outside, whenever the weather permitted. Rebecca's mother came in the next day with an anxious query. She was concerned to hear from Rebecca that the children would be allowed to 'tinkle on the grass' (her own phrase) on fine days. The confusion (with peeing) had been created by the teacher's careless use of the unfamiliar school expression P.E. Rebecca wasn't foolish or ignorant: she was making the best sense she could within her present understanding and frames of reference.

Children acting on the world

Children who have had the freedom to learn through acting on the world, building their understanding by doing and reflecting on the action, will have the capacity to make their own decisions and to choose their own paths.

But not all children are given this kind of freedom. These children will learn not to work things out for themselves, not to make their own connections or their own sense of the world. They will learn what they are told, to learn by rote, without explanation, without understanding. They will learn to rely on memory to recall facts that have no grounding in experience.

Without understand, these children will grow to be followers of well worn paths, nervous of deviating from the norm, of doing something different, of trying things out, unable to see the risk of failure as a challenge and an opportunity.

What matters to children: making sense of the world

When children explore the questions of
KNOWING HOW, KNOWING WHERE, KNOWING WHEN, KNOWING WHO *and* **KNOWING WHY**
they are working on the life long project of understanding some very big ideas indeed,
for example:
CAUSE and EFFECT, TIME, MYSTERY, IDENTITY,
RECIPROCITY, MORAL RESPONSIBILTY, LIFE and DEATH.   Rich et al 2005:53

A book for children

Plum

by Tony Mitton

Plum is a collection of poems written from the child's perspective. Through his poetry Tony Mitton tries to make sense of puzzling questions, mysterious myths and legends, extraordinary facts, the worrying state of the planet. His poems invite children to think and help them make sense of the world.

> *Once, when my daughter was about four and her mother was gardening, she suddenly asked with great seriousness, "What is under the grass, mummy?" This question kept coming back to me and gradually grew into a poem.*   p.21

Mitton's work is testimony to the value he places on children's thinking.

> **Big ideas:** *a big idea in every poem*

A book for educators

Children's Thinking: Promoting Children's Understanding in the Primary School

by Michael Bonnett

This is a book for educators who want to think about thinking and understand understanding. What is the part that educators can play in developing children's thinking and in promoting understanding? Michael Bonnett sets about answering this question by taking a philosophical approach, introducing readers to some relevant thinkers and philosophers who have much to contribute to the topic.

Some of the thinkers he discusses are more familiar than others; to meet Rousseau, Dewey and Piaget in a book about children's thinking is only to be expected. It is less predictable and a great deal more challenging to read about, for example, Martin Heidegger's distinction between 'calculative' and 'poetic' thinking. But Bonnett's careful exposition of the value and importance of poetic thinking is valuable and important in itself. It is through this kind of thinking and understanding that both educators and children develop the

> *...capacity to enter into the very being of things themselves, to be affected by them, to apprehend the underlying qualities of the human world.*   p.138

Review

These are the main themes of chapter U.

- However hard educators work on their behalf, children do the work of understanding by and for themselves.
- Children work to understand big ideas, the world and everything in it; in this process, handling, doing and talking come before abstraction and generalisation.
- The educator's responsibility is to attend respectfully to children's growing understanding, and to provide generously for their full-time project of making sense of everything they encounter.

What do learners do?
Learners *voice* **their learning**

"I am, I can, I have something to say"

I AM	I CAN
From birth children tell us of their essential being... ***I AM, I FEEL, I SUFFER, I LOVE, I REACH OUT, I TOUCH, I EXPLORE, I EXPERIMENT, I MAKE MEANING.***	*As children grow so do their powers to act on the world...* ***I CAN*** *ask questions about it* ***I CAN*** *make connections between different bits of it* ***I CAN*** *tell you which bits fascinate me* ***I CAN*** *talk about all these things I do.* Rich et al 2005:48

So listen to me

Children are constantly making maps, not geographical maps, but maps of their ever changing understanding. Every time children encounter a fresh experience they include it in their map, matching it with previous experience so that it makes sense.

In a lively study of children's invented spellings, Gunther Kress describes how James, aged seven, shows his understanding of the life-cycle of frogs.

> *When frogs are born there called frogs born and there in littel rond bits of jelly so they con't do nofing.*

James has not made a spelling mistake with *frogs born*. He has in fact spelt both words correctly. He is making sense of the birth of frogs. Kress points out that,

> *His solution is to take meaning as his key... it is about how frogs are born... Spelling here is indistinguishable as an activity from thinking about vocabulary, grammar and meaning.*
>
> *2000:41*

With so many experiences available to them, rich, diverse, confusing, contradictory, exhilarating, troubling and puzzling as many of them are, children are eager to share their perceptions and their growing understanding. They can do this in many ways: through their talk, questions, drawing, modelling, writing, when they make stories and play. But they need an audience to listen to their voices: a loving, observant, listening, responsive audience, otherwise there will be no-one to hear them, no-one to value their developing world maps.

Someone to hear

At the end of a school day, children leave their classes and head for home. The headteacher's door is open and as they make their way to the school front door, some children pop in.

First is Jane, aged nine, who doesn't realise the headteacher has a visitor and apologises very politely for interrupting. She is welcomed warmly. She has just come to say that she has had a good day, a happy day. For Jane, this is not always the case.

Next comes eight year old Evaline, newly arrived from Lithuania, to share a poem she has written for her mother. She reads it aloud to an appreciative audience, sharing her joy in her achievement.

These children know that someone will hear their voices. They are building their understanding of the way the world works. They are learning what is right and wrong, good and bad, kind and unkind; they seek affirmation from a loving adult.

Being heard

Amy, aged eight, has difficulty arriving at school in time for the start of the day. She cannot seem to get up. One morning she did not arrive until 11 o'clock, distressed and tearful. Her teacher commented that it must be very uncomfortable to arrive when everyone else had already started the day.

Nicholas listened to this exchange.
That afternoon after school he took his pocket money and bought an alarm clock. He gave this to Amy the next morning. Now she arrives on time. She knows that her voice has been heard, that what was said mattered to Nicholas, and that now it is up to her.

Where can children's voices be heard?

Who will hear my voice?

Wayne was a seven year old member of a small discussion group of eight or nine children who met regularly with their headteacher to discuss topics of interest to them. One day, the group was examining a long, narrow, paper bag they had noticed in the headteacher's room and speculating about its usefulness and purpose (it had originally contained a full-sized umbrella). One of the many suggestions that the children made was that the bag could have been designed to wrap a golf club. This idea roused Wayne to great excitement and eloquence. "A golf club! You can't say a golf club!" (spoken with the utmost scorn). "You can say a putter. Or a number four iron. But you can't say a golf club!" And so on, through a complete catalogue of the correct professional terms.

Children reverse the role

Some children appreciate the need to be an audience for others, as the two examples below show. The first, a conversation between Keelan aged ten, and his headteacher:

HT: Are you all right Keelan?
K: Yeah, are you?
HT: Yes, thank you.

The second, an exchange between a headteacher and 11 year old Danielle.

On the day of the opening of the new school building everyone was preparing the public spaces for the arrival of important visitors. The headteacher was busy hurrying from room to room, checking that everyone knew the programme for this momentous event. As she left the classroom, Danielle beckoned to her. "You need to do your hair" she whispered quietly. "Oh dear, Danielle. What's the matter with it?" asked the headteacher. "It's just a bit scruffy", said Danielle with gentle concern that her teacher should not let herself or the school down on this great day. A few minutes later the headteacher returned and standing in the doorway she just pointed to her hair with her eyes lifted in query. A thumbs up from Danielle and she left, reassured that she was presentable.

These children know that voicing concern for another's well-being is not a one way ticket from adult to child. They can reciprocate. Their voices are valued.

This outburst came as a great surprise to Wayne's teachers, who knew nothing of his regular weekend occupation as assistant caddy on the local golf course. The teachers' knowledge of Wayne was more narrowly drawn: there was a shared concern about his relative lack of achievement in reading and writing, and some anxiety about his behaviour in the playground. It was with both joy and humility that his teachers were obliged to reconsider their judgements of Wayne, and to re-think their approach to him as a learner. The chance discovery of Wayne's considerable expertise and experience did wonders for his reputation, and his mortified teachers treated him with a new respect, painfully aware of how limited their previous estimates of his learning capacity had been.

Where can children's voices be heard?

Without much difficulty and with little or no expense educators can provide a range of opportunities where children's voices can be heard.

...in their play
When children choose their own play themes, they have the opportunity to try many voices.

> What is it like to be in charge?
> To be responsible, compassionate, gentle, left out, hurt, afraid, fierce?
> Who decides on the role each child will play?
> Who negotiates for change?

Using their home and community languages in play, children can contribute, feel valued and develop their sense of belonging to the group.

...when they explore questions worth asking.
Questions worth asking are provocative starting points for debate and discussion. They will lead to hypothesis, deduction and valuing others' points of view.

There is probably no right or wrong answer: they stimulate creative imagination and lead children out into the real worlds of biology, physics, history, engineering and astronomy and into the inner worlds of philosophy, empathy and psychology.

When this question, from Thanos aged six, was added to a class display of work about forces it generated further thinking by the whole class, "I would like to know if there is a force that isn't a push or a pull".

...in their commentaries on their learning
Classrooms increasingly include commercially produced materials designed as learning aids. These can intrude on the space to the exclusion of the children's own work. When space is made to display children's work accompanied by their own commentaries, the classroom display becomes a dynamic reflection of children's thinking. This is even more powerful when the comments are made in the languages of children in the group. Everyone's voice is valued.

A question from a child is written in a display of work relating to a recent unexpected snowfall: 'Why is everything quiet when it snows?'

A title given by four year old Chloe to her weaving: 'Everything is so, so soft.'

In some classes children spontaneously write in their home or community language. In one class of eight year olds, children wrote stories in English and illustrated them before making them into books. Their stories were then translated into three other languages to reflect the voices of all the children in the class. There was a set of books in Cantonese, Urdu, Gujarati and English. Children could choose to read in any of the four languages.. They were very proud of the multi-lingual library full of their own stories.

...when they have a forum for talk: contributing to a collective voice

Children need places where they can exchange ideas, value different points of view, discuss, debate, wonder, make decisions, act on them and evaluate the outcomes. Some children may feel happier to express themselves through the collective voice of other people rather than speaking as an individual. Others enjoy the opportunity to be heard.

...when they read books that invite comment, such as: Frederick by Leo Lionni

Reeny and Frederick

In *The Girl with the Brown Crayon* (1992), Paley describes the growing relationship between five year old Reeny and the work of author Leo Lionni, particularly with Frederick the field mouse. Paley records the conversations between Reeny and her friends as they discuss the reaction of the other mice to Frederick's unusual behaviour. There is much debate about the generosity of the mice and their acceptance of Frederick's own contribution. In Paley's kindergarten children have a forum where their voices are heard. They listen to each other and try out their ideas; the attentive audience of their educator fosters both their capacity to contribute and their sense of belonging.

A book for children

Frederick by Leo Lionni

Frederick is a field mouse who chooses to collect a different kind of autumn harvest: he gathers colours and words, for the winter days will be dull and the field mice will run out of things to say to each other. The other mice are puzzled but respect Frederick's right to make his own collection. When winter comes and all the stores of grain are finished, they turn to Frederick. He entertains them with his power to create colourful pictures in the mind: he tells wonderful poems and stories to distract them from the hardships of winter.

This story portrays the behaviour of a mouse who is apparently selfish and does not pull his weight. Children can imagine the feelings of the other mice as they see Frederick sitting in contemplation while they hurry about their gathering. But as the story unfolds, children celebrate, with the field mice, Frederick's alternative contribution to the community.

Big ideas: the right to have a voice and a point of view respect for different view points

A book for educators

Assessment in Early Childhood Settings: Learning Stories by Margaret Carr

In this book Margaret Carr continues the story of the New Zealand curriculum document Te Whāriki, published in 1996, described in chapter J. Carr shows how the four agreed principles for early childhood curriculum, which have statutory force, have been used as the basis for a statutory assessment framework. Assessment practices in New Zealand:

- ❧ *enhance children's sense of themselves as capable people and competent learners*

- ❧ *reflect the holistic way that children learn*

- ❧ *reflect the relationships between the child, people and the learning environment*

- ❧ *involve parents, guardians and, where appropriate, the extended family.*

To readers and educators on the other side of the world, such statements may seem ambitious, aspirational, but hardly practical. In New Zealand,

on the contrary, these principles are not for sale; there is no alternative. They are the basis for the New Zealand approach to assessment, now known as 'learning stories', a narrative approach, which Margaret Carr vividly describes with copious examples of living, learning children. The dominant metaphor of this approach is story, not levels, targets, goals or standards.

Each child's learning is documented day by day in individual books; each child's story is, by definition, different, but all learning stories share certain characteristics. They take a credit, not a deficit approach to learning; they take a holistic view, they are not sub-divided into areas, skills or aspects of learning; they include children's learning at home, as well as in the setting; they document progression – over time the stories become longer, broader, deeper. They are used and valued in the settings as a valuable resource, not least by the children themselves, who love their learning stories and those of their friends. They carry them home in the evenings for their parents and grandparents to read, enjoy and make their own additions.

Review

These are the main themes of chapter V.
- ❧ When children's voices are valued, they encounter the important big ideas of individuality, difference and respect.
- ❧ Unless children's voices are valued, they are unlikely to reflect on their learning.
- ❧ As children voice their learning they make sense of the world and build their own world maps.

What do learners do?
We learn with friends

'I' and 'WE'

At an international conference in 2006, two of the authors of *First hand experience: what matters to children* presented a paper describing the underlying principles of their work. During the discussion, the point was forcefully made, by an eloquent and excited delegate, that the apparent emphasis in the publication on 'I', the active learner, 'at the heart of the process', in Plowden's memorable phrase (CACE, 1967), was only part of the story. Too much attention, as she saw it, to 'I', the single, solitary, independent learner, would distract educators from attending to 'WE', the company of friends, the community of learners who learn together, with and from each other.

The authors were prompt to acknowledge the force of her argument; learners are indeed, in turns, both individuals and members of pairs, threesomes, all kinds of friendship groups. Educators who attend to *what matters to children* will attend to all these kinds of learning. Their provision will be responsive to the activities of both 'I' and 'WE'.

Working with friends: the importance of 'we' in learning

Molly, aged six, could read and write with some independence, but remained resolutely silent during the plenary session of the literacy hour. However she had great energy and enthusiasm, and was, in her teacher's words, 'a formidable classroom organiser.'

The class had been tending caterpillars for several weeks and literacy hours were dominated by non-fiction texts about the the life-cycle of the butterfly. One day Molly's teacher suggested an extra challenge for independent literacy work: to make as many words as possible from 'caterpillar'. Molly was first to the whiteboard; by the end of the session she had discovered 29 words. The next day Molly used her organising skills to involve other children in the search. The small group generated 64 words, and challenged the class of six and seven year olds next door to do better.

For two more days children in Molly's class made seven different lists before reaching a grand total of 73 words. But there was one more list to come which was different from all their others.

This list showed the names of all the children who contributed to the final complete word list. But unlike all the other lists, list, each of the 11 names was joined by the word 'and'. The class teacher wrote

> This original device is the children's solution to the problem of how to express their collaboration and authorship. The repeated use of 'and' makes this list more than just a list; it becomes a statement of their work together for a real-life literacy purpose, a declaration of their collaboration... the contribution and inclusion of each member of the group is credited and linked by the firm, repetitive 'and'. [...] It is an affirmation of the importance, to them, of what they achieved together. The children knew that their list of names, linked by 'and', was a declaration of copyright, their proud right to be acknowledged authors of the work.
>
> Hanke 2002:85-6

These young children do not know that in the adult world, the authors of multi-author books conventionally list themselves without the multiple use of 'and', substituting the unspoken comma until the final ampersand. There is no earthly reason why they should be aware of this convention. What is so impressive is that they have invented a convention of their own, which distinguishes this list of collaborators, who are bound together in their joint enterprise, from the lists of individual 'caterpillar' words, which enjoy no such bond.

The repeated 'and's are a magnificent illustration of the importance of 'we' in learning.

Nat and James and Josh p and Jonathan and Jacob and Jasmine and Georgina and Stephen and Kerry and Gemma and Kerry and Juliette and Lucy and Sam b

Friends are valued by children

Best friends Ricky and Lee, aged seven, were playing a game of Yu-gi-oh cards at playtime. Lee took two of Ricky's cards and ran off, leaving Ricky so shocked and hurt that he went to his teacher. Lee was very ashamed and unhappy and hid in the corner of the classroom, refusing to speak to anyone. He knew he had been insensitive and hurtful.

The headteacher talked to Lee about what he had done. In her office Lee admitted that he had done a bad thing; that he had hurt his friend and he wanted to apologise. His class teacher was contacted and he brought Ricky so that Lee could talk to him about ways of repairing the distress he had caused.

Lee decided he should give Ricky one of his own Yu-gi-oh cards as compensation. His teacher asked him which card it should be, one he could easily spare or one of his best cards. Lee decided that the card to choose should be one that Ricky particularly wanted.

Ricky accepted the card and the apology with the words, "I am glad to have my cards back, but most of all I am glad to have Lee as my friend again, because you see, he is my guide-line."

Learning about friendship with friends in play

In play, children explore what it is like to be a friend of others and have friends. They test out the ways in which friends care for each other, provide for each other, have fun together, keep each other safe and resolve conflict. Together children explore and test out a variety of questions about friends. What is it like to be a friend? What is it like to have a friend? Is a friend always a friend? Are all friends good to have? Is it okay to be cross with a friend? How does it feel to lose a friend or find a lost friend? Can a friend ever be an enemy?

Being with friends is not always easy for children. Some have 'roller coaster' friendships and can find it hard to maintain stable relationships. While this can be very disturbing for them, it is an important part of learning how to disagree or disapprove while still remaining friends. Through their play children learn about the complexities of friendship and the many emotions associated with friendship.

Playing with others not only helps to build an understanding of friendships but is also a time when friendships can develop.

Dolls house play: learning from a community of small-world resources

Pre-school educator Laura was dissatisfied with the quality of small-world play in her setting, especially play with the dolls house. It was finely furnished and peopled with a large family, but it never seemed to engage children in sustained, complex play. Laura considered how she could extend and enrich children's experiences in this area of provision.

Two weeks later, Laura was thoroughly delighted with the success of her intervention, which was brilliantly simple. She had reorganised the distribution of resources in the setting so that the once solitary dolls house became part of a street, with other houses on each side of it. Without further ado, the row of three houses had become the stimulus for sustained, collaborative, complex play. Friends came together to the row of houses in twos and threes, to invent dramatic stories for the inhabitants of the street; there were parties, burglaries, weddings, quarrels and every kind of visiting between the busy households. The quiet lonely house had become a neighbourhood, where there was plenty to do, and see, and talk about.

What a wonderful example of children's capacity to express, in their play, their spontaneous impulse towards friendship and togetherness. The educator's inspired provision and reorganisation created opportunities for play that beautifully matched this capacity.

What is important to children when learning with friends?

"Although Millie is only eight months you can see that she likes being with people. She loves it when her sister Kate makes her laugh. And Mille gets very animated Kate's friends are here. You can see her trying to get their attention and be noticed. It's like she wants to be part of their gang."
Mother of eight month old Millie

"Learning with friends means you can get all the ideas together. You help each other to think better and friends can cheer you up."
Harrie, aged ten

"I like my friends. Being with friends is best. Mostly we play mums and dads. I JUST REALLY LIKE MY FRIENDS!"
Katie, aged four

"James is my best friend because we like the same things. He's good at maths and sometimes he helps me. But I can help him do building things. I'm really good at it, but it's best when we work together. You can build much higher things. You see, you need a 'holder' and a 'builder' sometimes to get it really good."
Alex, aged eight

"It's much better learning with friends. I DEFINITELY prefer it." Alice, aged eleven

"I like learning with friends better than on my own. When you're with friends you don't have to do things on your own. I do things with my friends- the stuff on the table and we do it together, and in the home corner too. You need friends when you pretend to be a scientist. You can't really be a scientist on your own because you need other scientists to help you do the scientist thinking."
Grace, aged six

Exploring big ideas with friends

Learning with friends gives children opportunities to explore big ideas that include:

trust	empathy	intimacy
sharing	fairness	inclusion
being part of a team	giving and receiving	partners and partnership
justice and injustice	jealousy	enemies
love	hate	

Exploring what matters to children with friends

Being with friends matters to children

And what do children do with their friends? Among other things, they:

theorise, exchange ideas	agree and disagree
comfort, console, celebrate	compete and collaborate
consider, negotiate, tolerate, plan together	support, help and listen to each other

The educators' role

To provide

places and spaces for friends	time for friendship	purposeful activities for friends

To organise opportunities for friends to be together

making	playing	planning
watching and listening	cooking	gardening
caring	celebrating	investigating
laughing		

A book for children

The Sleeping Sword by Michael Morpurgo

Bun Bendle has a terrible accident that leaves him blind. He feels that life will offer him no more adventures. But with the love and support of his loyal friends he builds a new life, and embarks on an extraordinary adventure in the kingdom of his hero, King Arthur.

Big ideas: community
despair
fate
friendship
loyalty
perseverance

A book for educators

The Kindness of Children

by Vivian Gussin Paley (1999)

Paley's detailed, moving and insightful observations and reflections of children in a London nursery, kindergartens, elementary and high schools in America, explore deep meaning in the behaviour of children towards one another.

Paley paints a convincing picture of children's spontaneous interest in each other, their genuine concern for friends, classmates and children everywhere, their abhorrence of unkindness and their desire for inclusion. In particular, she describes children's responses to one boy, Teddy, who is severely handicapped, showing how children learn kindness with and from each other. She develops this theme by showing how educators can learn to value and make use of children's remarkable gifts: their curiosity about others, their care for eachother and their rejection of all mean behaviour.

Those new to Paley's writing will be moved and motivated by her poetic charm and skills as an observer and story teller. She captures the stories children tell, and explains their reactions to each other, as they make sense of their mutual relationships and responsibilities. Paley is humbled by children who generously help their peers manage the injustices of school life and their teacher's (sometimes unkind) decisions.

The genius of Paley reveals how much, how often, how deeply children learn with friends.

Review

These are the main themes of chapter W.

When children learn with their friends, they are doing more than enjoying each others' company; they are active, intellectually, socially, emotionally. They are learning to agree and disagree, to comfort and to celebrate, to compete and collaborate.

What do learners do
Learners expect the help and truthfulness of grown ups

The title of this chapter is taken from an essay by Loris Malaguzzi in a passage where he discusses how the inner force that drives children's learning is greatly enhanced when they are convinced that their friends and the adults in their lives are precious resources.

Reggio Children 1996:30

"Well, I wonder"

Sally Schweizer (2007) points out that, 'Children look up to us [adults] for enlightenment.' They need honesty from adults, but honesty is only helpful if it is framed within the realm of their experience and understanding.

Schweizer asks, 'Do we need to answer all their questions straight away?' and suggests

> If they seem too difficult, we might leave a space and they answer themselves. 'Well, I wonder,' encourages a creative response, fitting many an unanswerable question and leaving the child happy as we wonder at the marvel together. In time the child will find an academic answer, as yet out of reach.
>
> p.10

Children who are left such a space by their educators can test out their own hypothesis, tackle issues in an open-ended way; take time to wonder.

Being helpful

Being helpful doesn't mean doing children's thinking for them. Adults are not helpful if they leave no room for children to flex their creative muscles or act on their own inspiration. The right kind of help comes in different forms, including a generous environment, described throughout this book. Another kind of help is rooted in detailed observations of children

> ...through the regular practice of systematic observation, educators learn to value the learning that they see going on before their eyes... They will be able to use their observations to plan their next steps, taking account of children's growing understanding and expanding horizons, and matching their plans to children's interests and concerns.
>
> Rich et al 2005:10

> If children know things, they're not afraid. They know about dangerous things too.
>
> Pre-school child quoted in Malaguzzi 1995:.22-23

Responding to difficult questions

> Children's difficult questions can be a challenge for educators and parents but dismissing them and hoping they will go away doesn't help children.
>
> Being helpful and truthful means:
>
> > listening to these [children's] questions attentively, without making assumptions or judgements and without blaming or scolding the children
> > sometimes saying that you don't know, but are prepared to find out or give it more thought
> > supporting and encouraging children in thinking through the effect of their words and actions on others, seeing how words can hurt, and how the 'kindness of children' can prevail.
> >
> > Rich et al 2005:75

"What is it like when you are dead?"

On their way home from school one day, eight year olds Claire and Samantha walked through a graveyard. A few days later they played together after school and there was unusual silence. Their childminder called for them, worried they had left the house. When she found them they were lying flat on the floor, parallel to each other, motionless. Claire complained, "Don't disturb us. We're being dead." Then she sat up and asked, "What is it really like when you are dead?"

This genuine question might be a case for the adult to reply, 'Well I wonder', or 'I don't honestly know', or 'I'll give it more thought.'

Stories for help and truthfulness

It would be easy to assume that the most helpful and truthful books are information books, but stories can help children get to grips with human understanding and their own experiences. Make-believe is a source of both help and truthfulness.

Fantasy: help or hindrance?

Seven year old Evie asked her parents, "When we go on holiday will a tsunami come? Will we all drown?" Taken aback, her mother replied, "We'll be all right if we have a magic stone." During the holiday they duly collected magic stones. Two months after their return from Indonesia Evie rediscovered one of the magic stones. She became very upset, crying, "Oh no, oh no. I've taken a magic stone. I should have left it for the tsunami people. That's why they all died. Too many children took their magic stones."

A less than truthful response can sometimes lead children into thinking they can do the impossible. Evie needed a different kind of reassurance, more helpful than magic stones; she needed to know about early warning systems, tsunami safety procedures and how unlikely tsunamis were in their holiday region.

Martin, aged three also had a magic stone which he proudly showed to his childminder when he played with plastic dinosaurs, saying, "This will keep me invisible from the mighty T. Rex." The stone offered him a satisfying solution to his anxiety about dinosaurs.

A book for children

The Garden by Dyan Sheldon

Jenny finds a curious stone while digging in her garden. Her mother explains that it is a flint arrow head, made hundreds of years ago. Her mother's stories about the people who made the arrowhead stir Jenny's imagination. She dreams of them as she sleeps out in the garden in her tent. In her dream the people who once lived in her garden return and talk to her around the camp fire. On waking, she still feels in touch with them; she reburies the flint in the earth where she found it.

This beautifully illustrated story is about making sense of the world, not only through experiencing it at first hand, but with the help and truthfulness of a grown up.

> **Big ideas: time**
> **touching the past**
> **belonging**

A book for educators

To Kill a Mockingbird by Harper Lee

Set in the American Deep South in the 1930s, Harper Lee's moving novel describes life in a racist, hypocritical society through the voice of a child, Scout. She and her brother Jem struggle to understand the difficulties faced by their father, Atticus Finch, a lawyer known for his integrity, in defending a young black man.

The children need honest answers to their difficult questions. Surely grown ups are always right? How can an innocent man be found guilty? Why can't their father save him?

Review

These are the main themes of chapter X.

- Children are entitled to consider big and important issues. Unless they live and learn in a generous environment they are unlikely to do so.
- Educators have the responsibility to value children's difficult questions and take them seriously.
- Helpful, truthful educators give explanations that children can build into their world and moral maps.
- Children often know more than adults think they know.

What do learners do?
Yippee!!! *learners love learning*

I'm a real writer!

11 year old Matheus comes from Brazil. He loves to write and can now do so in two languages. There is a Writing Club at his school, for children who choose to write, who believe in themselves as writers. Matheus was invited to join the club. His response was spontaneous and ecstatic.

Dear miss Mier

I will **LOVE** to go to writing club,
Miss Myer you are jus like a angle a you made my dream come true.

Writing
Club

Matheus de Almeida

Phoebe reaches out

The following extract from the novel, *The Memory Keeper's Daughter* by Kim Edwards, tells of Phoebe, a baby of 11 months with Downs syndrome, exultantly reaching and grasping for the first time. Caroline, her loving mother figure, watches.

Phoebe was making soft sounds, reaching. Her hands were brushing against Al's neck, his collarbone, his dark plaid shirt… Phoebe's hands were reaching for the medallion. Not batting at air, as she had this morning, but using Al's chest for resistance, her small fingers scraping and scraping the medallion into her palm until she could close her fist around it. Rapt with success, she yanked the medallion hard on its string, making Al raise his hand to the chafing.
Caroline touched her own neck too, feeling the quick burn of joy.
'Oh yes,' she thought. 'Grab it, my darling. Grab the world.'

p.104-105

New astronomers

A class of ten year olds visited a planetarium one evening where they met an astronomer who talked with them about the night sky. He took them outside to look at stars and planets; they used telescopes in the observatories. Walking back to the coach, two boys discussed the experience. One said, "That man, that astronomer… he has changed my life." His friend pondered on the experience for a while and then and agreed.

Off and away...

Anna was so proud of her new bike. She could hardly wait to ride it and set off on her first cycle ride, with her father steadying her with his hand on the saddle. "Don't look down," he advised. "Look up, as far ahead as you can see." Anna lifted her head. She pedalled faster and suddenly she was away, riding alone. Yippee!

Children reflect on singing in a school choir

Singing makes me happy.

I just LOVE singing.

I really like working with my friends.

The sound we make is awesome.

Singing is uplifting.

Book for children and educators

Hooray for Diffendoofer Day!

by Dr Seuss with help from Jack Prelutsky and Lane Smith

Every child should live in Dinkerville and go to Diffendoofer School where learning is active and varied. The children love their educators who, alongside the joyful activity, provide a curriculum for thinking, which even enables the children to face, with confidence, the unexpected and fearful TEST.

This story came to light after Dr Seuss died in 1991. He had wanted to write a book about a school teacher who was 'different-er than the rest'. Two of his friends, a writer and an artist, made his dream a reality.

> Miss Bonkers rose. "Don't fret!" she said...
> "I'm certain you'll succeed.
> We've taught you that the earth is round,
> That red and white make pink,
> And something else that matters more –
> We've taught you how to think."

Review

These are the main themes and big ideas of chapter Y.

- ❧ Belonging to a community of learners is essential for worthwhile learning.
- ❧ With the right kind of provision, children learn to think for themselves.
- ❧ Being engaged with authentic purposes matters to children.
- ❧ With the help of wise educators, learning is joyful.
- ❧ Learners love learning.

What do learners do?
zzzzz... educators sleep on it

This is the final letter of our alphabet and gives us an opportunity to revisit and re-emphasise the key characteristics of our approach to children's learning, just as we did in the final pages of *First hand experience: what matters to children.*

Children as learners	Nourishing food for active learners	Metaphors for learning
Acting on the world, touching and tasting it, exploring it, asking questions about it, comparing and contrasting, listening and looking, collecting bits of it, discussing and debating it. These are: **the verbs of learning**	Living animals and plants, natural materials, intriguing and useful artefacts, interesting people of all ages, big ideas, puzzling ideas, contrasts and consequences, identity and differences. These are: **the nouns of learning**	Not a ladder...nor a long-jump... by which learning can be calibrated, quantified or measured better to think of an exploration, a journey, a narrative: **learning stories**

On these last pages, we turn our attention to children's educators and their capacity to learn. Stenhouse, whose work was discussed in chapter P, wrote that

> ...*a good classroom is one in which things are learned every day which the* **teacher** *did not previously know.* [emphasis added]   1975:37

We can adopt and adapt this insight and argue that the best settings for children's learning are ones where the educators too do learning every day, just as the children do. And educators' learning, like children's, takes time. Educators' thinking, like children's, takes time: they all need time to think.

But this thinking cannot simply be done during one-off-day conferences or two hour staff meetings or training sessions. It has to be done slowly, over long periods of time; hence the need to sleep on it.

This book is not an attempt to do educators' thinking, or learning, for them. That is, in any case, impossible. Educators, like children, are in charge of their own thinking and learning. We have designed this book as a tool to think with; it is intended to stimulate educators to do particular kinds of thinking, and to remind them that there are important choices to be made:

- ❧ about children
- ❧ about the curriculum they deserve
- ❧ about learning.

Thinking about children

Gunilla Dahlberg and her co-authors explain the importance of such choices.

> We have choices to make about who we think the child is and these choices have enormous significance since... they determine the institutions we provide for children and the pedagogical work that adults undertake in these institutions.
> Dahlberg et al 1999:43

What does this claim mean in practical terms?
It means that:

- ❧ *If educators think of children as destructive, they won't let them handle precious objects or use sharp knives.*

- ❧ *If educators think of children as fragile, they won't let them climb trees or go out in the rain.*

- ❧ *If educators think of children as undiscriminating, they won't let them near a hot stove or offer them the right materials to clean up with.*

- ❧ *If educators think of children as ignorant they won't appreciate the learning they have been doing from birth, the learning that matters to children.*

In short, educators can choose between a deficit approach, seeing children as intellectually weak, immature and incompetent; or they can take a credit approach, as the educators in Reggio Emilia do, and conceptualise children as rich, strong and powerful. Not materially rich, not physically strong or politically powerful, but rich in ideas and invention, strong in feeling and in friendship, powerful thinkers and intrepid explorers of the world. If educators choose to think of children in this way, they can provide openings into big ideas, introducing them to the conceptual richness of the world. By which we do not mean early lessons on the rivers of Africa or the capital of Brazil; we mean the richness of the natural world, the world of made things, the world of books, the world of people and ideas.

Thinking about learning: to have or to be

Here too, there are choices to be made. Is learning a thing to *have*? Something to accumulate, as targets are reached, goals achieved and levels tidily ticked off? Or is learning more like living? This book is emphatically about learning as *being*, the characteristics of being an active learner, an extended discussion of *what learners do*. Attending to *what learners do*, to the processes of learning, will make educators more effective than attending to the outcomes or end-points of learning. Learning is not a ladder, up which, rung by rung, learners must go. Learning is a way of being in the world, belonging, desiring, imagining, making meaning and understanding.

Thinking about curriculum

This was the central theme of *First hand experience: what matters to children*, in which we argued that children deserve a curriculum that matters to them, a curriculum that engages their emotions and challenges their thinking. In his fine book, *Primary Understanding* (1988), Kieran Egan, an eminent educator and thinker, urges educators to construct a curriculum 'made up of important content that is rich in meaning for children.'

The responsibility for constructing such a rich, meaningful curriculum, for making the right choices of experiences, materials, resources, is, we believe, squarely in the hands of children's educators. However many official well-intentioned bodies there may be who attempt to tell the professional educational community what to do, in ever more excruciating detail, we argue that there is no reason for educators to stand meekly back and allow themselves to be dictated to. We want educators to reclaim their responsibility to think for themselves about curriculum, and to use the fruits of that thinking in the interests of children.

Learning then, is very different from achievement. And it is far more important to look at learning, than it is to look at levels of achievement or attainment, for a number of reasons.

- *All children learn, all the time. Whereas not all children attain some of the specified levels at the prescribed ages or formal assessment points. (Some children learn to read at the age of three, and some at seven.)*

- *Focussing on attainment, the end-point of a process, can distract educators from learning, the ongoing process.*

- *An over-emphasis on the concept of attainment, we believe, can limit educators' understanding of learning.*

- *A focus on attainment at some point in the future relegates the here-and-now, children's daily experiences, to being a means to an end, rather than worthwhile educational ends in themselves.*

- *Attainment in the distant future is not the most useful criterion for evaluating the quality of children's lived experiences, their active, daily learning, which should be, as Egan argues, important learning, rich in meaning.*

Using this book to think with

We hope that educators of children from birth to 11 will use this book to think with.

To think about what, precisely?

About children as learners, about what learners do.

And about their own learning as educators.

Educators as learners

Educators' learning with this book will be of different kinds:

- learning about big ideas and the four domains of children's learning: what matters to children

- learning to evaluate the quality of their provision and organisation

- learning that not all learning is worthwhile

- learning to articulate their own underpinning principles

- learning about the richness of what all learners do.

Above all, educators who think deeply about all these things

- learn to make wise choices in the interests of children.

Nourishing food for educators

Every page of this book has been designed to feed and stimulate educators' thinking: the analysis of what active learners actually do, the snappy quotations from significant thinkers, the learning stories, the reviews of research studies, the accounts of children's play, the essays on Dewey, Noddings and Stenhouse, the libraries of books, the summaries of books for children and educators.

The outcomes of learning

We hope that educators who read this book will find it supports their learning of many kinds, especially in building a joined-up understanding of *what learners do*, a coherent, articulated, working model of children's powers. Understanding the key elements of our approach will enable educators to apply their learning, in ways of their own invention, to every dimension of their practice.

And finally...

we hope that when educators read this book

it will convince them of what we call

the 'yippee factor'...

Learners play

A Learners learn *all the time*

B Learners **belong** to a community of learners

C Learners choose

D John Dewey: experience and education

E Learners learn *everywhere*

Learners play

F Learners feel

G Learners need a generous environment

H Learners hope

I Learners imagine

J Learners do joined-up learning

K Learners know more than adults think they know

L Learners need libraries of books

M Learners make meaning

N Nel Noddings: learning to care

O obedience versus desire in learning

P principles of procedure

Q Learners question and answer

R Learners represent their learning

Learners play

S Learners make stories

T Learners take time

U Learners thirst for understanding

V Learners voice their learning

W We learn with friends

X Learners expect the help and truthfulness of grown ups

Y Yippee! learners love learning

Z Zzzz... educators need time to sleep on it

...children love learning

116

REFERENCES

Books for educators

Alcott, L.M. (1871) *Little Men* Boston: Roberts Brothers

Alexander, R. (2006) *Towards Dialogic Teaching: Rethinking classroom talk* Dialogos (third edition)

Anning, A., & Ring, K. (2004) *Making Sense of Children's Drawings* Maidenhead: Open University Press

Armstrong. M. (1980) *Closely Observed Children* London: Writers and Readers

Armstrong. M. (2006) *Children Writing Stories* Maidenhead: Open University Press

Ashton Warner, S. (1963) *Teacher* London: Secker & Warburg

Athey, C. (1990) *Extending Thought in Young Children* London: Paul Chapman Publishing

Atwood, M. (1990) *Cat's Eye* London: Virago

Axline, V. (1990) *Dibs in Search of Self* London: Penguin Books (first edition 1969)

Barrie, J.M. (1921) *Peter Pan and Wendy* London: Hodder & Stoughton

Bettelheim, B. & Zelan, K. (1982) *On Learning to Read: The Child's Fascination with Meaning* New York: Vintage Books

Bonnett, M. (1994) *Children's Thinking: Promoting Children's Understanding in the Primary School* London: Cassell

Booth, T. & Ainscow, M. (2002) *An Index for Inclusion: developing learning and participation in schools* Bristol: Centre for Studies on Inclusive Education

Bruce, T. (1987) *Early Childhood Education* London: Hodder Education (new edition 2005)

Carr, M. (2001) *Assessment in Early Childhood Settings: Learning Stories* London: Paul Chapman

Castagnetti, M. & Vecchi, V. (eds) (1997) *Shoe and Meter* Reggio Emilia: Reggio Children

Claxton, G. (2002) *Building Learning Power* Bristol: T.O.L. Ltd

Central Advisory Council for Education (1967) *Children and their Primary Schools* London: HMSO (The Plowden Report)

Cook, H. Caldwell (1917) *The Play Way An Essay in Educational Method* London: William Heinemann (reprinted in 1966 by Cedric Chivers Ltd.)

Cooper, P., Drummond, M.J., Hart, S., Lovey, J. & McLaughlin, C. (2000) *Positive Alternatives to Exclusion* London: RoutledgeFalmer

Cuffaro, H.K. (1995) *Experimenting with the world: John Dewey and the Early Childhood Classroom* New York: Teachers College Press

Dahlberg, G., Moss, P. & Pence, A. (1999) *Beyond Quality in Early Childhood Education and Care: Postmodern Perspectives* London: Falmer Press

Davies, B. (1989) *Frogs and Snails and Feminist Tales: PreSchool Children and Gender* Sydney: Allen & Unwin

Day, K. (1995) One Moonlit Night in *A Boxful of Stories* Hertford: Hertfordshire County Council

Department for Education and Skills (2007) *Practice Guidance for the Foundation Stage* Nottingham: DfES

Department for Education and Skills (2007) *Statutory Framework for the Early Years Foundation Stage* Nottingham: DfES

Department of Education and Science (1985) *The curriculum from 5-16* London: HMSO

Department of Education and Science (1990) *Starting with Quality: The Report of Inquiry into the Quality of the Educational Experiences Offered to 3 and 4 Year Olds* London: HMSO (The Rumbold Report)

Desforges, C. (1992) *Children's Learning: has it improved?* Paper given at the Association for the Study of Primary Education (ASPE) national conference, Cheshire, 1992

Desforges, C. (2006) 'Learning and Development' Rich Learning Opportunities conference *First hand experience: what matters to children* (The Eden Project: Cornwall)

Desforges, C. & Coburn, A. (1987) *Understanding the mathematics teacher: a study of practice in first schools* London: Falmer Press

de Waal, E. (2005) 'The event of a thread, the event of clay: Black Mountain College and the Crafts' in *Starting at Zero Black Mountain College 1933-57* Arnolfini, Bristol & Kettle's Yard, Cambridge

Dewey, J. (1916) *Democracy and Education* New York: Macmillan

Dewey, J. (1958) *Art as Experience* New York: Capricorn Books (first edition 1934)

Dewey, J. (1963) *Experience and Education* London: Collier Macmillan (first edition 1938)

Dewey, J. (1990) *The School and Society* Chicago: University of Chicago Press (lectures given in 1899)

Dickens, C. (1854) *Hard Times* London: Bradbury & Evans

Doddington, C. & Hilton, M. (2007) *Child-Centred Education: Reviving the Creative Tradition* London: Sage

Donaldson, M. (2006) *Children's Minds* London: Harper Perennial (first edition 1978)

Drummond, M.J. (2003) *Assessing Children's Learning* London: David Fulton (second edition)

Dweck, C. (1999) *Self Theories: their role in motivation, personality and development* Philadelphia: Taylor & Francis

Edwards, C., Gandini, L. & Forman, G. (eds) (1998) *The Hundred Languages of Children: The Reggio Emilia Approach Advanced Reflections* Norwood NJ: Ablex Publishing Co.

Edwards, K. (2005) *The Memory Keeper's Daughter* New York: Penguin

Egan, K. & Nadaner, D. (1988) *Imagination and Education* Milton Keynes: Open University Press

Egan, K. (1988) *Primary Understanding* London: Routledge

Featherstone, S. (ed) (2006) *L is for Sheep: getting ready for phonics* Leicester: Featherstone Education

Fisher, D.C. (1913) *A Montessori Mother* London: Constable

Fromm, E. (1942) *Fear of Freedom* London: Routledge & Kegan Paul

Fromm, E. (1956) *The Sane Society* London: Routledge & Kegan Paul

Furbank, P.N. (1992) *Diderot: A Critical Biography* London: Minerva

Gardner, D. (1969) *Susan Isaacs The First Biography* London: Methuen

Goethe, J.W. von (1970) *Theory of Colours* Cambridge, Mass: The MIT Press

Goldschmeid, E. & Jackson, S. (1994) *People Under Three* London: Routledge

Griffiths, R. (1930) *A Study of Imagination in Early Childhood* London: Routledge & Kegan Paul

Haddon, M. (2003) *The Curious Incident of the Dog in the Night-time* London: Jonathan Cape

Halliday, M.A.K. (1973) *Explorations in the Functions of Language* London: Edward Arnold

Hanke, V. (2002) Improvisations around the National Literacy Strategy *Reading* 36 (2) 80-87

Hardeman, M. (1974) *Children's ways of knowing: Nathan Isaacs on Education, Psychology and Piaget* New York: Teachers College Press

Harlen, W. (1977) *Match and Mismatch: Raising Questions* London: Oliver & Boyd

Hart, S., Dixon, A., Drummond, M.J. & McIntyre, D. (2004) *Learning without Limits* Maidenhead: Open University Press

Hodgson Burnett, F. (1911) *The Secret Garden* London: The Phillips Publishing Company

Hohmann, M., Banet, B. & Weikart, D. (1979) *Young Children in Action* Ypsilanti: High/Scope Press

Holm, A. (2004) *I am David* Orlando, Fla.: Harcourt (first edition 1963)

Holmes, E (1911) *What Is and What Might Be* London: Constable

Holmes, E. (1920) *In Quest of an Ideal* London: Constable

Holmes, G. (1952) *The Idiot Teacher* London: Faber & Faber (reissued by Spokesman 1977)

Holt, J. (1990) *How Children Fail* London: Penguin (first edition 1964)

Hughes, A. (2006) *Developing Play for the Under 3s* London: David Fulton

Hughes, M. (1989) The Child as a Learner: The Contrasting Views of Developmental Psychology and Early Education in Desforges, C. (ed) *Early Childhood Education British Journal of Educational Psychology* Monograph Series No. 4 Edinburgh: Scottish Academic Press

Isaacs, S. (1930) *Intellectual Growth in Young Children* London: Routledge

Isaacs, S. (1932) *The Children We Teach* London: University of London Press

Jackson, P. (1968) *Life in Classrooms* New York: Holt, Rinehart & Winston

Jackson, P. (1998) 'Dewey's Experience and Education Revisited' in Dewey, J. *Experience and Education: the 60th Anniversary Edition* West Lafayette, Indiana: Kappa Delta Pi

Jefferies, R. (1882) *Bevis: The Story of a Boy* London: Sampson Low

Jenkinson, S. (2001) *The Genius of Play* Stroud: Hawthorn Press

Kipling, R. (1901) *Kim* London: Macmillan & Co Ltd.

Korczak, J. (2005) *King Matt the First* London: Vintage (first edition 1923)

Kress, G. (2000) *Early Spelling: between convention and creativity* London: Routledge

Lane, J. (2006) *Right From The Start* Wiltshire: Focus F.I.R.S.T. [Focus Institute on Rights and Social Transformation]

Lee, H. (1960) *To Kill a Mockingbird* London: Heinemann

Levertov, D. (2003) *New Selected Poems* Northumberland: Bloodaxe Books

Lifton, B.J. (1989) *The King of Children* London: Pan Books

Lindon, J. (2001) *Understanding Children's Play* Cheltenham: Nelson Thornes

MacDonald, G. (1871) *At the Back of the North Wind* London: Strahan & Co.

Malaguzzi, L. (1995) *A Journey into the Rights of Children* Reggio Emilia: Reggio Children

Manning, K. & Sharp, A. (1977) *Structuring Play in the Early Years at School* London: Ward Lock

Mark, J. (2003, April 26) *Children's books review* The Guardian

Marshall, S. (1963) *An Experiment in Education* Cambridge: Cambridge University Press

Martin, J.R. (1992) *The School Home: Rethinking Schools for Changing Families* Cambridge, Mass: Harvard University

Martin, J.R. (1994) *Changing the Educational Landscape: Philosophy, Women and Curriculum* London: Routledge

Matthews, J. (2003) *Drawing and Painting in Early Childhood, Children and Visual Representations* London: Paul Chapman (first edition 1994)

Meek, M. (1988) *How texts teach what learners learn* Stroud: Thimble Press

Ministry of Education (1996) *Te Whãriki Early Childhood Curriculum* Wellington NZ: Learning Media

Morpurgo, M. (2007) *Singing for Mrs Pettigrew: a story-maker's journey* London: Walker Books

Neil, A.S. (1962) *Summerhill* London: Victor Gollacnez (published by Pelican Books 1968)

Nobel, A. (1991) *Educating Through Art: The Steiner School Approach* Edinburgh: Floris Books

Noddings, N. (2002) *Educating Moral People* New York: Teachers College Press

Noddings, N. (2005a) *The Challenge to Care in Schools: An Alternative Approach to Education* New York: Teachers College Press

Noddings, N. (2005b) Identifying and responding to needs in education *Cambridge Journal of Education* 35 (2) 147-159

Nutbrown, C. (1999) *Threads of Thinking: Young Children Learning and the Role of Early Education* London: Paul Chapman (second edition)

Opie, I. (1993) *The People in the Playground* Oxford: Oxford University Press

Paley, G. (1985) *Later the Same Day* Harmondsworth: Penguin

Paley, V.G. (1979) *White Teacher* Cambridge, Mass: Harvard University Press

Paley, V.G. (1981) *Wally's Stories* Cambridge, Mass: Harvard University Press

Paley, V.G. (1984) *Boys and Gilrs: Superheroes in the Doll Corner* Chicago: University of Chicago Press

Paley, V.G. (1988) *Bad Guys Don't Have Birthdays* Chicago: University of Chicago Press

Paley, V.G. (1990) *The Boy Who Would Be A Helicopter* Cambridge, Mass: Harvard University Press

Paley, V.G. (1993) *You Can't Say You Can't Play* Cambridge, Mass: Harvard University Press

Paley, V.G. (1997) *The Girl with the Brown Crayon* Cambridge, Mass: Harvard University Press

Paley, V.G. (1999) *The Kindness of Children* Cambridge, Mass: Harvard University Press

Paley, V.G. (2001) *In Mrs. Tully's Room: A Childcare Portrait* Cambridge, Mass: Harvard University Press

Paley, V.G. (2004) *A Child's Work: The Importance of Fantasy Play* London: Heinemann

Paley, V.G. (2005) *Personal correspondence*

Piaget, J. (1951) *Play, Dreams and Imitation in Childhood* London: Heinemann

Pullman, P. (1996) Pullman Carnegie Medal Acceptance Speech, England

Reggio Children (1996) *The Hundred Languages of Children* (exhibition catalogue) Reggio Emilia: Reggio Children

Rich, D., Casanova, D., Dixon, A., Drummond, M.J., Durrant, A. & Myer, C. (2005) *First hand experience: what matters to children* Clopton: Rich Learning Opportunities

Rico, G.L. (1983) *Writing the Natural Way* Los Angeles: Jeremy P. Tarcher

Rinaldi, C. (2006) *In Dialogue with Reggio Emilia: Listening, researching and learning* London: Routledge

Roberts, R. (2002) *Self-Esteem and Early Learning 0-8 Years* London: Paul Chapman Publishing (second edition)

Robinson, M. (2003) *From Birth to One: the year of opportunity* Buckingham: Open University Press

Rudduck, J. & Hopkins, D. (eds) (1985) *Research as the Basis for Teaching: readings from the work of Lawrence Stenhouse* London: Heinemann Educational Books

Sachar, L. (1998) *Holes* London: Bloomsbury

Schiller, C. (1979) in Griffin Beale, C. (ed) *Christian Schiller in his Own Words* London: A. & C. Black

Schweizer, S. (2007) *Well, I Wonder! Childhood in the Modern World, A Handbook for Parents, Teachers and Carers* Forest Row: Sophia Books

Seuss, Dr., Prelutsky, J., & Smith L. (2001) *Hooray for Diffendoofer Day!* London: Harper Collins

Southgate, V., Arnold, H. & Johnson, S. (1981) *Extending Beginning Reading* London: Heinemann Educational Books

Spufford, F. (2002) *The Child that Books Built* London: Faber & Faber

Stenhouse, L. (1975) *An Introduction to Curriculum Research and Development* London: Heinemann Educational Books

Tanner, R. (1987) *Double Harness* London: Impact Books

Tizard, B. & Hughes, M. (1984) *Young Children Learning: Talking and Thinking at Home and at School* London: Fontana

Tobin, J. J., Wu. D. & Davidson, D. (1989) *PreSchool in Three Cultures* New Haven: Yale University Press

Toogood, P. (1984) *The Head's Tale* Telford: Dialogue Publications

Tough, J. (1976) *Listening to Children Talking* London: Ward Lock

Twain, M. (1884) *The Adventures of Huckleberry Finn* New York: Charles L. Webster & Co.

Van Ausdale, D. & Feagin, J. (2001) *The First R – How Children Learn Race and Racism* Lanham, Maryland: Rowman & Littlefield

Warnock, M. (1986) 'The education of the emotions' in Cooper, D. (ed) *Education, Values and the mind* London: Routledge & Kegan Paul

Waters, M. (2007) A curriculum tonic! *Early Education* 51.7-8

Watson, F. (1996) I can...I do...I understand *Community Works Journal* Spring

Weil, S. (1986) Prerequisite to Dignity of Labour (an essay written in 1941) in Miles, S. (ed) *Simone Weil: an anthology* London: Virago

Wells, G. (1987) *The Meaning Makers: Children Learning Language and Using Language to Learn* London: Heinemann

Welty, E. (1985) *One Writer's Beginnings* London: Faber & Faber

Willes, M. (1983) *Children into Pupils* London: Routledge & Kegan Paul

Williams, E.M. and Shuard, H. (1970) *Primary Mathematics Today* London: Longman

Winterson, J. (2007, November 3) The Guardian

Wolfenberg, P.J. (1999) *Play and Imagination in Children with Autism* New York: Teachers College Press

Wood, D., McMahon, L. & Cranston, Y. (1980) *Working with the Under Fives* London: Grant McIntyre

Books for children

Base, G. (2001) *The Water Hole* New York: Abrams

Bodkin, O. (1998) *The Crane Wife* Orlando USA: Harcourt Books

Bradman, T. (2001) *Daddy's Lullaby* London: Bloomsbury

Brighton, C. (1999) *Fossil Girl* London: Frances Lincoln

Brown, R. (2000) *Snail Trail* London: Andersen Press

Cooper, S. (2003) *Frog* London: Red Fox

dePaola, T. (1988) *The Legend of the Indian Paintbrush* New York: Hutchinson

Geraghty, P. (2002) *The Hunter* London: Red Fox

Gonsalves, R. (2005) *Imagine a Day* New York: Atheneum

Hoban, R. (2002) *How Tom Beat Captain Najork and His Hired Sportsmen* London: Red Fox (first edition 1974)

Hoffman, M. (2002) *The Colour of Home* London: Frances Lincoln Ltd.

Lionni, L. (1971) *Frederick* London: Hodder & Stoughton

Lobel, A. (1971) *Frog and Toad Together* London: Harper Collins

McAfee, A. (1998) *Why do Stars Come out at Night?* London: Red Fox

McLerran, A. (2004) *Roxaboxen* London: Harper Collins

Mitton, T. (1998) *Plum* London: Scholastic Press

Morpurgo, M. (2002) *The Sleeping Sword* London: Egmont Books

Morpurgo, M. (2005) *I Believe in Unicorns* London: Walker Books

O'Brien, R.C. (1971) *Mrs Frisby and the Rats of Nimh* New York: Atheneum

Pitcher, C. (1998) *The Time of the Lion* London: Frances Lincoln

Say, A. (1993) *Grandfather's Journey* New York: Houghton Mifflin Company

Sheldon, D. (1993) *The Garden* London: Hutchinson

Stockton, F.R. (2003) *The Bee-man of Orn* London: Walker Books

Townley, R. (2001) *The Great Good Thing* London: Simon & Schuster

van Allsburg, C. (1984) *The Mysteries of Harris Burdick* New York: The Houghton Mifflin Co.

First hand experience: **what matters to children**
by Diane Rich, Denise Casanova, Annabelle Dixon, Mary Jane Drummond, Andrea Durrant, Cathy Myer

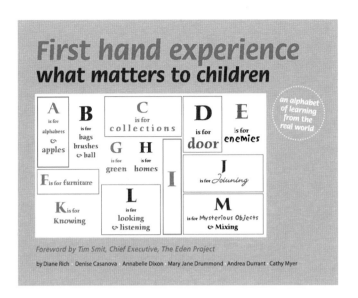

"Read this book. It may save lives."
Tim Smit, chief executive, The Eden Project

"Altogether a remarkable achievement and I cannot recommend 'First hand experience' highly enough. It is a work of genius."   Sue Palmer, author and consultant

"This is the only book out there that is challenging our thinking and making a difference to what goes on in schools and early years settings."   Headteacher

"Every page is an adventure. I keep it with me for inspiration and power."
Teacher

"This has revitalised the curriculum I work with and made me see that it's not a straightjacket at all. It's really enriched everything I do with children."   Early years educator

"This book is the first and only book I have ever seen that places this vital and natural relationship with the real world through real experiences, at the heart of an apporach to learning. The book is a pleasure to use, created to inspire and lead teachers. A must for every staff room."   Museum educator

"This book captures the essence of how children best learn. It inspires and influences deep as well as being a practical guide for all those involved in children's learning. It should be a 'must read' and 'do' and 'be' for all!"   Educator

"In days when children are becoming increasingly static in classrooms and schools this wonderful book reminds us of the importance of first hand experiences. Children have become increasingly passive and lack opportunities to demonstrate their amazing creativity. Through this book teachers are inspired to think about 'what matters to children' and change their practice as a result. There are stimulating conferences that are led by the authors that inspire and remotivate tired teachers."   Educator

Copies are available from Rich Learning Opportunities
The Brambles
Manor Road
Clopton
Suffolk
IP13 6SH
United Kingdom

www.richlearningopportunities.co.uk • office@richlearningopportunities.co.uk
ph +44 (0)1473 737405 • fax +44 (0)1473 737613

The **What Matters to Children** team is a group of well-respected education consultants co-ordinated by **Rich Learning Opportunities**. They have come together to write books, develop and deliver conferences and training sessions based on the publications and the principles which underpin their work.

Rich Learning Opportunities was formed by Diane Rich in 2004 aiming to keep creativity, play and first hand experience at the heart of children's learning.

The authors of *Learning: what matters to children*, Diane Rich, Mary Jane Drummond and Cathy Myer are members of the **What Matters to Children** team. The other team members are:

Denise Casanova, Jacqui Cousins, Andrea Durrant, Emma Hertzberg,
Jennie Lindon, Marjorie Ouvry, Sue Pearson, Jane Turner.